FRANK B. GILBRETH, JR.

AND

ERNESTINE GILBRETH CAREY'S

Cheaper by the Dozen

Jackie

DRAMATIZED BY

CHRISTOPHER SERGEL

Mike

Levin

THE DRAMATIC PUBLISHING COMPANY

*** NOTICE ***

Cheaper by the Dozen

A Comedy in Three Acts

FOR NINE MEN AND SEVEN WOMEN

CHARACTERS

MR. GILBRETH . . . . *Dad*
MRS. GILBRETH . . . . *Mother*
ERNESTINE
FRANK
JACKIE
DAN
BILL . . . . *part of their dozen*
FRED
ANNE
LILLIAN
MARTHA
MRS. FITZGERALD . . . .*the housekeeper*
DR. BURTON . . . .*the family doctor*
JOE SCALES . . . .*a cheerleader*
MISS BRILL . . . .*a teacher*
LARRY . . . .*someone "special"*

PLACE: *The living-room of the Gilbreth home, Montclair, New Jersey.*
TIME: *The twenties.*

SYNOPSIS

ACT I: *Scene 1:* The Gilbreth living-room. A day in Autumn.
Scene 2: The same. Two weeks later.

ACT II: The same. A few weeks later.

ACT III: The same. A day in Spring.

NOTES ON CHARACTERS
AND COSTUMES

THE GILBRETH CHILDREN: The children range in age from seventeen on downward. Anne is the oldest; then come Ernestine, Martha, Frank, Bill, Lillian, Fred, Dan, and Jackie. The actual ages of the children can be left to the discretion of the director, depending on the availability of casting material. For the effective use of stage business it is suggested that the children's sizes be graduated from the tallest on down in height to Jackie, the shortest. If it is desired to use costumes of the 1920's, the boys may wear knickers, shirts, sweaters, and long stockings. The girls dress conesrvatively in simple jumper dresses, middy blouses, and skirts, with long cotton stockings. Anne, in her gradual emancipation from this conservative type of dress, changes to silk stockings. As the play progresses she wears more colorful and grown-up clothes.

DAD: Dad is tall, and no longer slim. He carries himself with the self-assurance of a successful man who is proud of his wife, proud of his family, and proud of his business accomplishments.

MOTHER: Mother is a gracious, attractive woman. She is also a psychologist. In her own way, she is often able to get even better results with her large family than Dad, but she is not a disciplinarian. However, she never threatens, shouts, or becomes excited. She dresses neatly in the prevailing clothes of the period.

MRS. FITZGERALD: She is a buxom, kindly woman, and completely devoted to the family. Sometimes her patience is tried by the goings-on in the large household. She wears a house dress and apron.

DR. BURTON: Dr. Burton, the family doctor, is a plain, outspoken man. He wears a dark suit and carries a small black bag.

JOE SCALES: Joe is Anne's age, a very short, cocky chap. He wears a bright, horizontally striped sweater or blazer, loud pants, a bow tie, and pork-pie hat.

4

MISS BRILL: She is thin and sallow, with angular features, and wears the type of glasses that pinch together on the bridge of her nose. She wears a tailored suit. Miss Brill has no love for the children, and they have none for her.

LARRY: Larry is also Anne's age, a nice-looking, clean-cut boy. On his first appearance in Act Two he wears slacks and a sweater. Later in the same act he changes to his best suit. He again wears the slacks and sweater in Act Three.

CHART OF STAGE POSITIONS

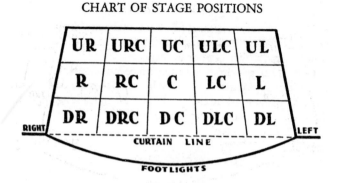

STAGE POSITIONS

*Up*stage means away from the footlights, *downstage* means toward the footlights, and *right* and *left* are used with reference to the actor as he faces the audience. R mean *right*, L means *left*, U means *up*, D means *down*, C means *center*, and these abbreviations are used in combination, as: U R for *up right*, R C for *right center*, D L C for *down left center*, etc. One will note that a position designated on the stage refers to a general territory, rather than to a given point.

NOTE: Before starting rehearsals, chalk off your stage or rehearsal space as indicated above in the *Chart of Stage Positions*. Then teach your actors the meanings and positions of these fundamental terms of stage movement by having them walk from one position to another until they are familiar with them. The use of these abbreviated terms in directing the play saves time, speeds up rehearsals, and reduces the amount of explanation the director has to give to his actors.

STAGE CHART

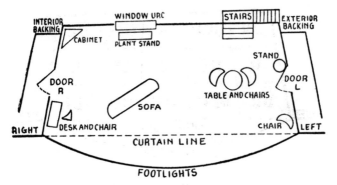

PROPERTIES

GENERAL: Sofa, pillows on sofa, round table and two comfortable chairs, vase on round table, large easy chair, umbrella stand, plants in plant stand, desk and chair, drapes on window, telephone on desk, tall corner cabinet or whatnot, rugs, lamps, pictures, various knickknacks, Anne's package in desk drawer containing piece of flimsy underwear and silk stockings (Act One), checkers and checkerboard (Act One), Dad's cane in umbrella stand (Act One).

DAD: Three large packages, stop-watch, five jackknives, four small manicure sets, watch, papers, large sheet of paper (cross-section graph).

MARTHA: Book.

ANNE: Manicure set, handkerchief, paper.

DAN: Dog.

BILL: Umbrella, sandwich.

MISS BRILL: Papers, pencil, pad.

FRANK: Thick manuscript.

ERNESTINE: Large floppy hat.

LILLIAN: Large lollipop.

LARRY: Nail-studded piece of board.

ACT ONE

The houselights fade out. Music is heard playing softly. It is "Love's Old Sweet Song." The curtain has not yet risen. A dim spotlight opens up at D R stage, revealing a girl and boy standing in front of the curtain. If possible, only their heads and shoulders are visible in the spotlight. They are listening intently to the music. When they speak, it is in a quiet, reminiscing way.]

ERNESTINE. Can you hear the music, Frank? I think it's coming from down the street.

FRANK. I thought I heard something else.

ERNESTINE. Songs like that make you remember.

FRANK. I thought I heard a whistle—like Dad used to whistle assembly call.

ERNESTINE [*smiling at him*]. How could you hear that? [*A distinctive whistle is heard from off L stage.*]

FRANK. There! [*Glances at* ERNESTINE, *but she shakes her head. He feels he must be mistaken, and half shrugs it away with a smile.*] Funny how a sound stays with you.

ERNESTINE. It's Dad that stays with you.

FRANK [*with affection*]. Because he had enough gall to be divided in three parts. Mother said the day the United States entered the First World War, Dad telegraphed President Wilson—"Arriving Washington seven P.M. If you don't know how to use me, I'll tell you how."

ERNESTINE [*defensively*]. He showed them how to save time assembling machine guns.

FRANK. But you couldn't tell where Dad's scientific management ended and his family life began. [*Smiles.*] Even buttoning his vest from bottom to top to save four seconds.

ERNESTINE [*with pride*]. But he could walk into the Zeiss

9

works in Germany or the Pierce Arrow plant in this country
and announce he'd speed up production one-fourth—and
then do it.

FRANK [*imitating Dad, speaking decisively*]. "And what works
in the factory will work in the home!" [ERNESTINE *smiles.
After a pause.*] I guess with so many of us, it was scientific
management or bedlam.

ERNESTINE. Even with a dozen, I don't think Dad was satis-
fied. I remember him looking us over, and then saying to
Mother: [*Imitates him, shaking her head.*] "Only twelve.
But never mind, Lillie, you did the best you could."

FRANK. Remember when Mother came home from a trip and
asked him if everything had run smoothly? He told her:
"Only had trouble with that one over there—[*Points.*]—
but a good spanking brought him into line." Mother had to
say: "That's not one of ours, dear. He belongs next door."

ERNESTINE [*smiling*]. I remember. [*Pause, as she listens.*] The
music coming from down the street. We used to sing that
song.

FRANK [*nodding*]. Three-part harmony.

ERNESTINE. The whole family rolling along in the Pierce Arrow, singing "Love's Old Sweet Song." Dad'd lean back
against the seat and cock his hat on the side of his head.
Mother would snuggle up against him as if she were cold. I
remember her turning around once between songs and saying: "Right now is the happiest time in the world."

FRANK [*quietly, remembering*]. Maybe it was.

ERNESTINE [*haltingly, as she thinks it*]. Maybe that's the time
in a family—when you're all together—before anything's
happened to any one of you.

FRANK [*repeating thoughtfully*]. "Right now is the happiest
time in the world." Remember when she said it again?

ERNESTINE [*nodding*]. Dad with his bad heart—leaving to
lecture at the World Management Conference in Europe. He
was about to go, and he whistled assembly call. We came
running and we were all together. It was the last time. Dad

was trying to hug us all, and then Mother said it. [*There is a momentary pause as they both remember. The music grows fainter and soon fades out entirely.*]

FRANK. When I think of Dad, I don't think of that. [*With increasing warmth and force as he speaks.*] I think of him color-chalking our fingers and the typewriter keys so even the babies were learning the touch-system, or taking movies of us washing dishes so he could analyze them and eliminate waste motions.

ERNESTINE [*nodding*]. Painting diagrams on the wall to show the solar system—or the difference between meters and yards. Tapping out messages in Morse code—telling those that understood where candy was hidden.

FRANK. And how he hated distractions. Remember how he used to shout at those two noisy canaries?

ERNESTINE [*nodding*]. The one he named, "Shut up," and the other, "You heard me." [*The curtain begins to rise, and the spotlight starts to fade.*]

FRANK. But the way I remember Dad best—he'd come bounding up the front steps with his arms full, and he'd be busting to try out some new idea. He'd come roaring into the living-room, take out his stop-watch, and whistle assembly call. That meant—come running.

[*The curtain is up. The living-room of the Gilbreth home is large, comfortable, with a well-lived-in appearance, and furnished in the style of the period. The door to the outside is L, while a door R leads to the dining-room and kitchen. In the rear wall, U L C, three steps lead to a landing, and then a flight of stairs turns left and continues on up to the second floor of the house. There is a large draped window in the rear wall, U R C. In front of it is a large stand for potted plants. Below the door R are a desk and chair. On the desk is a telephone. At an angle at R C is a sofa, while at L C stage are a round table and two comfortable chairs. There is another large easy chair D L. Above the door L is a stand for*

umbrellas. A tall corner cabinet or whatnot is in the U R
*corner of the room. Rugs, lamps, pictures, and knickknacks
complete the setting.* DAD *has come through the door* L *with
his arms loaded with three large packages. He sets these in
the chair* D L *and takes a stop-watch out of his vest pocket.
He crosses to* C *stage, gives a loud, distinctive whistle, and
clicks the stop-watch. He doesn't look up from the watch as
young people come from all directions.* ANNE *and* MARTHA
hurry in R. BILL *and* LILLIAN *come tearing down the stairs.
The window* U R C *is thrown open and* FRED *scrambles in.*
JACKIE *dashes down the stairs tucking in his shirt as he
comes.* DAN *rushes in* L *and slams the door on a dog that has
been barking after him. He opens the door again to shout,
"Go on home," to the dog, and then hurries across to the
others.*]

ALL [*as they line up at an angle in front of sofa*]. I'm first,
after you! That's doesn't count! Out of my way! You're in
my place! What is it, Dad? Don't push me! Hello, Dad!
[FRANK *turns to* ERNESTINE, D R, *where they are still standing.*]

FRANK. Didn't you hear Dad whistle?

ERNESTINE. I wasn't sure.

FRANK. Come on. We're late. [*The spotlight goes out as they
cross to the others and squeeze into their positions in line.
The* CHILDREN *quiet down, and straighten the line. Starting
with the smallest, who is farthest downstage, the line builds
in height to the tallest at the other end of the line, upstage.
Through all this,* DAD *hasn't raised his eyes from the stop-
watch. The moment* FRANK *and* ERNESTINE *are in place,* DAD
clicks the watch and his head snaps up.]

DAD. Fourteen seconds.

FRANK [*cheerfully*]. That's pretty good. [DAD *glares at him.*]

FRED. Only eight seconds off the record.

DAD. Where's your mother?

ANNE. Upstairs with the babies.

DAD [*gruffly, moving in front of table* L C]. I had so many children because I thought anything your mother and I teamed up on was certain to be a success. Now I'm not so sure. [*Whirls abruptly.*] Let me see your fingernails.

LILLIAN. What, Daddy?

DAD. Fingernails! [*All hands are thrust forward with fingers outstretched.* JACKIE *winces at sight of his own nails, jerks them back, and starts buffing them against his trousers.* DAD *moves down line like a hard-to-please general making an inspection.*] Not very clean—need trimmings—looks like you've been biting them. [*As he reaches* JACKIE.] Jackie! [JACKIE *holds out his hands reluctantly.* DAD *shakes his head mournfully at the sight.*] Look at those nails! [JACKIE *bows his head over his nails, inspecting them at a range of two inches.*] What do *you* think of them? [JACKIE *shakes his head mournfully in echo of his father.* DAD *brightens and reaches into one of his bulging pockets.*] What you need is a jackknife to keep your nails clean. [*Hands jackknife to* JACKIE.]

JACKIE [*wide-eyed*]. Gosh, Dad!

DAD [*smiling, passing them out*]. All you boys need jackknives —[*To* GIRLS.]—and I've some little manicure sets for the girls. Here—here's yours. [*Pulls a small manicure set from pocket.*]

CHILDREN [*clustering around him, as he empties his pockets*]. Thank you, Dad. Golly, thanks! Look at mine! A real stag handle! There's scissors—and a file. What a beauty! Thanks, Dad—thanks!

DAD [*sternly*]. I'll inspect your nails again. [*Picks up packages he left in chair, looking about speculatively.*] Now where can I put these?

DAN. What's in those boxes?

LILLIAN. Is it something for us in those boxes?

DAD [*pretending not to understand*]. *These* boxes?

BILL. Come on and tell us.

DAD. It's something special—something interesting, and educational—but a lot of fun, too. [*Starts for stairs.*] I'll tell you about it tomorrow—or maybe the day after.

JACKIE. *Daddy!*

LILLIAN. Please! [CHILDREN *cluster about him at foot of stairs.*]

DAD. Next week sometime.

MARTHA. Tell us now.

ERNESTINE. You're going to anyway.

ANNE. You know you are.

DAD [*with a scowl*]. Since you insist. [*Comes to sofa as they troop after him, and sets packages down.*] These are two Victrolas and some records! [*He looks expectantly from face to face. Their expressions show definite disappointment.*]

FRED. But we have a Victrola.

DAD. Downstairs.

ANNE. Well? . . .

DAD. These Victrolas are for the upstairs bathrooms. One for the boys' bathroom. One for the girls' bathroom.

ERNESTINE [*in dismay*]. The bathrooms!

DAD [*trying to whip up enthusiasm*]. I'll bet we'll be the only family in town with a Victrola in every bath.

FRANK [*dolefully*]. That wouldn't surprise me.

DAD. I've been thinking about the time you waste in the bathroom. At first I thought it was unavoidable delay.

ANNE [*shaking her head*]. Here we go——

DAD [*happily*]. Then I thought of these Victrolas. [*Determined.*] You're going to play them every morning while taking baths, brushing teeth, washing faces——

ANNE. Why?

DAD. Does there have to be a "why" for everything?

ERNESTINE [*patiently*]. There doesn't have to be, but with you there always is.

ANNE. When you start talking about Victrolas, dance music

isn't the first thing that pops into our minds. [DAD *looks at them.* ALL *shake their heads.* ANNE *is right.*]

DAD [*with generous frankness*]. I admit it's not dance music.

ANNE [*ruefully*]. We might start thinking about dances.

MARTHA [*grimly*]. What kind of records?

DAD [*swallowing*]. Very entertaining, *and* educational. [ALL *look at him doubtfully. He bursts out.*] Language lessons. French and German.

CHILDREN. Oh, no! Please!

DAD [*his voice rising*]. You don't have to listen to them consciously. Just play them, and finally they'll make an impression.

ANNE. Not every morning in the bathroom!

DAD [*wheedling*]. I spent a hundred and sixty dollars for this equipment.

BILL. It's not even unwrapped. Maybe you could get your money back, Daddy.

DAD [*shouting*]. I don't want my money back. And if those Victrolas aren't going from the minute you get up till you come down to breakfast, I'll know the reason why.

DAN. One reason—it's impossible to change records while you're in the bathtub.

DAD. A person can be in and out of the tub in the time it takes a record to play. That's why you're taught motion study.

MARTHA. You didn't teach anything about taking a bath.

DAD [*beaming*]. Ahh! [*They asked for it.*] I'll now demonstrate how to take a bath without waste motions—without dabbing here and then there and taking an hour. [CHILDREN *groan.*] Dan and Fred, bring over that little rug. [*Indicates small throw rug near desk* D R.] We'll pretend it's a bathtub.

ERNESTINE. You mean—right now?

DAD. I mean, at once. [DAN *and* FRED *pick up rug and come toward sofa.*] Put it there. [*They place rug* D C, *where* DAD *indicates.* DAD *tosses a pillow from sofa on to rug, and carefully eases himself down on it.*] I'm in the bathtub. [CHIL-

DREN *crowd around him.* DAD *looks from face to face, as
though daring anyone to dispute the fact.*]
JACKIE [*mollifying*]. Yes, Daddy.
DAD. A little more hot water, Jackie. [JACKIE *turns on an imaginary faucet, and then turns it back.* DAD *feels imaginary
water.*] Ahh, that's fine! [*Looks at them.*] I have a cake of
soap in my right hand. Now, pay attention to this one simple,
continuous motion. [*Suits action to words.*] From the top of
the shoulder—down the top of the left arm, back up the
bottom of the arm, and then down the left side. Got it?
[CHILDREN *nod.*]

[*Unobserved,* MOTHER *starts down the stairs.*]

DAD. Shift soap. [*Lifts imaginary soap.* CHILDRENS' *eyes follow,
ALL heads turning in unison.*] Same motion. Other side. [*As
he starts,* MOTHER *crosses to him.*]
MOTHER [*humorously*]. Don't forget the back of your neck.
DAD [*rising, delighted to see her*]. Hello, Boss. I'm not forget-
ting a thing. [*Steps over side of imaginary bathtub.*]
MOTHER [*smiling*]. Glad you're home early. What's all the
racket?
DAD. Fingernail inspection.
MOTHER [*taking his hand affectionately*]. How about yours?
[*Shakes her head as she looks at them and speaks, half jok-
ing, half serious.*] Biting them again.
DAD [*spinning her hand around with his*]. Let's see yours. [*Sud-
denly concerned.*] I told you not to wash the dishes yourself.
MOTHER [*knowing* DAD *doesn't realize all the problems of
housework*]. There's already too much for the cook to do.
DAD. I'll take care of that. Just a matter of saving motions.
Dishes or bathing—it's all the same thing. [*Turns to* CHIL-
DREN, *in a lecturing tone.*] Continuing—give a little attention to your feet and the back of your neck, and you'll be out
of the tub before you can say "Bonjour." [*Dismisses subject
and them.*] Now you know all about taking a bath. Put the

rug back, and take the Victrolas upstairs. [*To* MOTHER.]
Now, Boss, I'll talk to the cook. [*Strides to door* R.]

MOTHER [*following him*]. We'll *both* talk to her. [*Goes out
R, after* DAD. LILLIAN *and* JACKIE *toss pillow on sofa and
replace rug* D R, *while* DAN, FRED, FRANK, *and* BILL *start upstairs with packages.*]

FRED [*to* DAN]. Grab on.

FRANK. Which goes in which bathroom?

BILL. We'll give the girls the French.

MARTHA. I much prefer French.

DAN. Jawohl!

LILLIAN [*hurrying up after* BOYS]. Is "Jawohl" French or German?

JACKIE [*following* LILLIAN *upstairs*]. I think it's Spanish.
[DAN, FRED, FRANK, BILL, LILLIAN, *and* JACKIE *are up the
stairs and out.*]

ANNE [*at* C *stage, in wonder*]. Dad has a system for everything.

ERNESTINE [*smiling agreement*]. Even conjugating French and
German verbs in the bathtub. [*Flops wearily on sofa.*]

MARTHA [*thoughtfully, sitting in chair right of table* L C]. If
he'd only think of a system for interesting a couple of boys
I know at school.

ERNESTINE. In what?

MARTHA. In me.

ANNE [*still standing at* C *stage*]. A person has to think of
some things for herself. [*With meaning.*] I did.

ERNESTINE. What do you mean?

ANNE. I'm going to have it out with him.

ERNESTINE. Have what out?

ANNE. Somebody has to, and I'm the oldest.

MARTHA. What are you going to do?

ANNE [*determined*]. I'm going to stop dressing like a freak.
Aren't you tired of all the boys thinking you're a freak?

ERNESTINE. Yes, but——

MARTHA. Dad says——

ANNE [*loudly*]. I don't care what he says.

MARTHA [*apprehensively, glancing* R]. He might hear you.

ANNE. He's going to, anyway. [*Thrusts out one leg.*] Cotton stockings! No wonder we never get asked anywhere. No boy would dare be seen with us. The way it looks, I'll be the only person to go through Montclair High without once being asked to a dance. [*Unhappily.*] Whenever the telephone rings, it's just some girl.

ERNESTINE. A boy called yesterday. [*They look to her in surprise. She continues lamely.*] He wanted my notes on the Second Punic War.

MARTHA. You'd think it would impress fellows—I mean, knowing things like the touch-system and the Morse code.

ERNESTINE. But it doesn't matter at all.

ANNE. I *had* to do something. [*Crosses quickly to desk and takes a package from drawer.*] I bought some things—up-to-date things like other girls wear. [*In a scared-but-glad tone, as she moves back to* C *stage.*] And they look absolutely snaky. [ERNESTINE *and* MARTHA *rise and move to her.*]

MARTHA [*as* ANNE *starts to open package, warningly*]. Careful —he might walk in any minute.

ANNE. Let him. I'm not a sneak.

ERNESTINE. What'd you get?

ANNE. Short underthings, and—[*Bravely.*]—silk stockings.

ERNESTINE [*catching her breath*]. Silk—stockings!

MARTHA. But when Dad . . . [*She is unable to finish.*]

ANNE. They're right in this package. [*Hugs package to her.*] And I'm going to wear them, and I'm going to be asked to dances, and lots of boys will want to dance with me. [*Gulps.*] And I'll be a really popular girl.

ERNESTINE [*joining the dream*]. And if he lets you wear them, he'll have to let me wear them, too.

MARTHA. And me!

ERNESTINE. And we'll all be having dates, and going to dances.

MARTHA. And we can talk over our different boy-friends, and compare notes, and——[*The dream is beautiful.*] Golly!

ANNE [*looking lovingly at her package*]. Silk stockings!

ERNESTINE [*with look towards door* R, *sharply*]. Anne! It's Dad!

MARTHA. Hide it! Quick!

[ANNE *rushes over to hide the package in the desk drawer as* DAD *and* MRS. FITZGERALD *enter* R, *followed by* MOTHER. DAD *comes to* C *stage, followed by* MRS. FITZGERALD *and* MOTHER. ERNESTINE *and* MARTHA *move quickly toward* D L.]

MRS. FITZGERALD. More efficiency—that's all I hear.

DAD. If you'd just apply motion study——

MRS. FITZGERALD. Motion study is fine as long as it's somebody else's motions you're studying.

MOTHER [*placatingly*]. You'd better get along with dinner, Mrs. Fitzgerald. My husband told you he'd take care of it.

MRS. FITZGERALD [*grumbling, as she moves* R]. Lincoln freed the slaves. [*Turns.*] All but one. All but one. [*Goes out* R.]

DAD [*to* MOTHER]. We'll handle this the same way we would in a factory.

MOTHER. It isn't exactly the same.

DAD [*decisively*]. Exactly. And what works in the factory——

MOTHER [*smiling*]. Yes, dear.

[DAD *takes out his stop-watch and whistles assembly.* FRANK, BILL, LILLIAN, FRED, JACKIE, *and* DAN *come pouring back down the stairs. The line is formed exactly as before.* DAD *clicks the watch and his head snaps up.*]

DAD. Twelve seconds. [*The* CHILDREN *look from one to the other, pleased with the good time.* DAD *continues, meaning to sell the idea.*] I've a wonderful surprise for you! We're going to try a wonderful new idea!

ALL [*excitement from* YOUNGER CHILDREN]. Tell us! What is it? Is it fun, Daddy?

MARTHA [*with a faint trace of suspicion*]. What kind of idea?

DAD [*with gusto*]. We're going to set up a family council. Your mother's not going to run this household any more. *I'm* not going to run it, either.

BILL [*wondering*]. Then who?

DAD [*enthusiastically*]. *You* are!

BILL [*misunderstanding, dumbfounded*]. Me!

DAD. *All* of us—through a democratic family council. We'll have a family democracy! Everybody votes. You'll be deciding things for yourselves. *You'll* work out the questions that come up. [*There is a general reaction of "That's great!"*]

DAN [*delighted*]. Gosh, Dad—we will?

DAD. You bet we will! You know how I get factories to set up joint employer-employee boards to make assignments on the basis of personal aptitudes? [*There is a general nod.*]

MARTHA [*not fooled entirely*]. Yes, but—what kind of assignments, Dad?

DAD. Every sort of assignment—this and that—even—[*Dropping word at last.*]—work assignments. [*There is a general deflation on the part of the* CHILDREN. DAD *catches this and tries to swing them back along with him again. He speaks quickly.*] Now! You're going to love this—and it's a great step forward. You'll see. The Gilbreth family council is going into session right now. Arrange yourselves. Frank, bring your mother a chair. We'll get right into the business before us. [FRANK *brings chair* D L *to* C *stage and seats* MOTHER.]

MOTHER [*in an aside, to* DAD]. Just like a factory? [*The* CHILDREN *quickly arrange themselves.* ANNE *sits in chair by desk* D R. LILLIAN, JACKIE, BILL, *and* MARTHA *squeeze together on sofa.* DAN *perches on right arm of sofa, while* FRED *perches on left arm.* ERNESTINE *sits right of table* L C, *and* FRANK *sits in chair left of same table. These positions are taken with split-second timing. Each one knows his or her place in these family meetings.*]

DAD [*confidently, crossing behind table* L C, *banging on table with vase*]. I now call this meeting to order. [*Explaining.*] That means—quiet. [*Hands are folded.* EVERYONE *settles back.* DAD *speaks formally.*] You'll notice I'm installed here as your chairman. I assume there are no objections. The chair, hearing no objections, will——

ANNE [*standing up*]. Mr. Chairman.

DAD. Out of order.

ANNE [*quickly*]. Since this is going to be a democratic council, I think the chairman should represent the common people.

DAD. You're very much out of order. The chair has the floor.

ANNE. But you said you heard no objections, and I want to object.

DAD [*flaring up*]. Out of order means you're out of order and sit down. [ANNE *sits as* DAD *glares at her. Then he continues.*] The first job of the council is to apportion the necessary work about the house. Does the chair hear any suggestions? [*There is a pause.* DAD *forces a smile.*] Come, come, fellow members. How do you want to divide the work? [*There is another blank silence.* DAD *looks helplessly to* MOTHER.]

MOTHER [*amused*]. I don't think anyone wants to divide the work or otherwise be associated with it in any way, shape, or form.

DAD [*turning back, sharply*]. In a democracy, everybody speaks. So start speaking. Dan, I recognize you. What do you think about it? I'm warning you—*speak!*

DAN [*rising*]. I think Mrs. Fitzgerald and Tom should do the work. They get paid for it.

DAD [*shouting*]. Sit down. You're no longer recognized. [DAN *stares about him.*] Bill, I recognize you.

BILL [*rising*]. I think Tom and Mrs. Fitzgerald have enough to do. [DAD *beams at him.* BILL *takes a deep breath.*] So I think we should hire more people to help with the work.

DAD. You're out of order, too. [*Turns to* MOTHER, *appealing.* BILL *sits.*] Boss, now what?

MOTHER [*to* CHILDREN]. Of course, we *could* hire more help. [CHILDREN *beam.* DAD *is startled.*] But that means saving somewhere else. If we cut out all allowances, moving pictures, new clothes, and so forth——

CHILDREN. Hey, Mother! No! Wait a minute!

DAD [*now beaming again*]. Ahh! Do I hear a motion to that effect? [*Looks expectantly from face to face.*] Who wants to stop allowances? Moving pictures?

MOTHER. Seriously, we'll all have to help.

FRANK [*after a pause, rising*]. I move the boys cut the grass and rake leaves. [*Sits.*]

ERNESTINE [*rising*]. And I move the girls sweep, dust, and do supper dishes. [*Sits.*]

MOTHER. And everyone makes his own bed.

DAD [*quickly*]. Except the chairman.

MOTHER. Except the chairman.

DAD. Second the motion. All those in favor? [*There is a murmur of "Aye."*] Opposed? Motion carried. There being no other business——

FRED [*jumping up quickly*]. Mr. Chairman, I understand the purchase of a new rug is intended.

MOTHER [*surprised*]. Yes—it is.

FRED [*with a dark look at MOTHER*]. Can the budget afford such a rug?

DAD [*surprised*]. Well—I don't know. [*Beaming, to MOTHER.*] Sounds to me as if they have a good point, Boss.

MOTHER [*testily*]. I planned to spend a hundred dollars.

FRED. I move no more than ninety-five dollars be spent. [*Sits again.*]

DAD. I second that motion, too. [*Still beaming.*] All those in favor? [*The "Ayes" have it.* DAD, *laughing, turns to* MOTHER.] I'm afraid you lose on that one, Boss. [*Turns to* CHILDREN.] Now, if there's no further business——

DAN [*hopping up*]. Mr. Chairman, I move we spend the five dollars we just saved to buy a collie puppy.

DAD [*shouting*]. Hey, wait a minute!

MOTHER [*with sidelong glance at* DAD]. Second the motion.

DAD. Out of order. Very much out of order.

JACKIE. A dog would be a pet. Everyone could pat him, and I would be his master.

BILL. A dog would sleep at the foot of my bed, and I would wash him when he was dirty.

DAD [*mimicking*]. A dog would be an accursed nuisance. He would be our master. Nobody would wash his filthy, flea-bitten carcass. He'd positively sleep on the foot of my bed.

DAN. Let's vote.

DAD. Any pet that doesn't lay eggs is an extravagance.

CHILDREN. Vote! Vote!

DAD. This council is adjourned! Meeting adjourned! That's all!

DAN. All those in favor? [*There is a thundering "Aye."*]

DAD [*thundering back*]. No!

MOTHER [*smiling, to* DAD]. I'm afraid you lose on that one, Boss. [DAN *sits again, smiling victoriously.*]

ERNESTINE. I think this council is a very good idea.

MARTHA. There're lots of things we should take up.

DAD [*outraged*]. I suppose next you want ponies, roadsters, trips to Hawaii—[*With increasing disgust.*]—silk stockings! [ER-NESTINE *and* MARTHA *both gasp and look at* ANNE, *who tenses up, with elbows pressing in at her sides.*]

ANNE [*standing up quickly, her expression that of one expecting a blow, her voice rising to a squeak*]. Mr. Chairman!

DAD [*irritably*]. What is it?

ANNE [*gulping*]. There is still further business I wish to place before the council.

ERNESTINE. And it's important.

ANNE. I'll—I'll show you. [*Turns and takes package from desk drawer.*] I'm not hiding a thing. I want the entire family to see.

DAD [*half smiling at this*]. Shall I bring down the babies?

ERNESTINE. Be serious. [ANNE *crosses to* DAD *behind table* L C.]

DAD [*suspiciously*]. What is it?

ANNE [*opening package, taking out a short, flimsy piece of un-derwear*]. To begin with—these underthings—these teddies. [*Faces him.*] I'm going to wear them. [BOYS *whoop at sight.*]

DAD [*horrified*]. You will not! Put them back in the box. It em-barrasses me even to look at them.

ANNE. I bought them with my own money.

DAD [*holding it up against himself; it is very short and he is shocked*]. You'll take this right back to the store. [*Thrusts it at her.*]

ERNESTINE. There's only one other girl in school besides us who doesn't wear teddies.

MARTHA. If you don't believe us, come to school and see for yourself.

DAD [*indignantly*]. That won't be necessary.

MOTHER. I'm glad there's one other sensible girl in school besides you.

ERNESTINE. But *she* doesn't even wear a teddy.

MARTHA. And if you don't believe us——

DAD. It still won't be necessary.

FRED. They're getting boy-crazy, Dad.

BILL. That's all they talk about.

FRANK. You should see them eyeing the boys in the hall at school, or in the lunchroom——

MARTHA. You little snakes!

LILLIAN [*to* BOYS]. Shame on you.

ANNE [*determined to see it through*]. You might as well know —it isn't just teddies. I bought—[*Swallows.*]—silk stockings. [*Holds one up.*]

DAD [*in absolute horror*]. No!

MOTHER. Anne! You didn't!

DAD [*taking stockings, slipping his hand inside, even more shocked*]. You might as well go barelegged as wear these! [*There is no answer. He continues angrily.*] You can see right through them! [*Pause, then shouting.*] They're like the last of the seven veils!

ANNE [*with a sigh of relief, moving over toward left end of sofa.*] Now you know.

DAD. Don't you realize what might happen if you go around showing your legs through silk stockings?

MARTHA [*interested, leaning forward*]. What?

DAD. Never mind.

ERNESTINE. But that's the way everybody dresses today.

ANNE. Boys don't notice when everyone dresses that way.

DAD [sharply]. Don't tell me about boys. I know all about what boys notice.

ANNE [in anguish]. You don't want us to be wallflowers?

DAD [righteously]. I'd rather raise wallflowers than clinging vines.

ANNE [clutching her package, with determination]. I'm going to wear these. [Intensely.] I'll not be a wallflower any more!

ERNESTINE. And I'm going to buy silk stockings, too.

MARTHA. And me.

DAD [roaring, banging on table]. I won't let you out of the house with them.

ANNE [pleadingly, crossing to him]. Don't you see, Dad? [Her cup of misery overflowing]. I've never even been asked to the drugstore for a plain, ordinary, vanilla soda!

DAD [reasonably]. If it's vanilla sodas you want——

ANNE [turning away]. Oh, Dad! [Moves toward MOTHER.]

DAD. As for boys, they don't get serious about the kind of girl who wears silk stockings. They just run around with them.

ERNESTINE [to DAD]. If you ask me, it's a dead give-away to be so suspicious. It denotes a misspent youth.

DAD [shouting]. Nobody asked you! [Crosses to ANNE.] Listen to me, Anne. When a man picks a wife, he wants someone he can respect.

ANNE [brushing past him, starting up the stairs, unhappily]. They certainly respect me. [Pauses on landing.] I'm the most respected girl in the whole school. The boys respect me so much they hardly look at me. [Starts upstairs.]

DAD. Come back down here! [As she doesn't, he shouts.] I don't want you wasting your time with a lot of boys! [Hopefully.] Look at the fun we have right here at home with our projects.

ANNE [pausing]. You don't understand! You don't understand at all! [In misery.] I wish your job was selling shoes, and you only had one or two children——[Voice rises to a wail.]—and neither of them was me! [Bites her lip and runs up rest of

stairs and out. There is a general murmur of surprise.
MOTHER *is looking at* DAD.]

FRANK [*to other* BOYS]. I guess we'd better start cleaning up the
yard. [*Rises.*] Come on.

ERNESTINE [*to* GIRLS]. Let's give a hand in the kitchen. [*Rises.*]

LILLIAN [*hopping up to lead the way*]. Okay.

MOTHER [*rising, patting* LILLIAN *on shoulder as she goes past*].
Good girls.

ERNESTINE. I'll straighten up the living-room. [*Crosses to door*
R *and pauses.* LILLIAN *and* MARTHA *go out* R. FRANK *pauses*
at door L *as* JACKIE, BILL, DAN, *and* FRED *go out* L.]

DAD [*to* MOTHER, *concerned*]. Boss—what is it I don't understand?

MOTHER [*briefly*]. High school girls.

DAD [*with a glance upstairs*]. Remember when we decided to
have a dozen children—remember what I suggested?

MOTHER. You suggested we have all boys.

DAD. I'm not blaming you, Boss, but you should have followed
my suggestion. [*Turns and starts upstairs, muttering.*] High
school girls! [*Determined.*] By jingo, there's only one way to
handle this. [*Strides upstairs.*]

MOTHER [*good-humoredly*]. Just like in a factory. [*Shakes her*
head slightly, then crosses and goes out R. *There is a pause,*
as the stage lights begin slowly to dim. FRANK, *who hesitated*
at the door L, *calls across to* ERNESTINE.]

FRANK [*in hushed voice*]. Hey—Ern?

ERNESTINE [*also speaking quietly*]. What, Frank? [*As they*
speak, they move D R, *to same position they were in at the be-*
ginning of play.]

FRANK. Why doesn't Dad want you wearing silk stockings and
having dates?

ERNESTINE. I don't know why.

FRANK. But Dad has a reason. I mean, he wouldn't do it without
a reason.

ERNESTINE. No. He wouldn't.

FRANK. But what could the reason be? [ERNESTINE *shakes her head. She doesn't know. They are now* D R. *The lights on the stage black out, and the spotlight picks them up, as before. Once more they speak in a reminiscing manner.*] Do you remember one time—[*Tries to recall.*]—I think it was after Dan bought the five-dollar dog—it was about two weeks after Anne first showed Dad the silk stockings.

ERNESTINE [*recollecting, with humor*]. I remember the battle over those stockings!

FRANK. But a little while after that—Dad and Doctor Burton had a long conference upstairs. Then they came down together, and Dad was joking.

ERNESTINE [*nodding, as she remembers*]. And we didn't think anything about it. We didn't even have a suspicion.

FRANK. That's the time.

ERNESTINE. They were so cheerful. Gosh, Frank—when a man with a dozen children gets told his heart's on the blink, what's he going to do?

FRANK. That's what I'm getting at. I mean, maybe that's why—maybe that's the reason he didn't want you girls thinking about boys and movies and sodas all the time.

ERNESTINE [*with a smile*]. It wouldn't contribute to skipping grades at school.

FRANK. Don't you see? The further we were along in school—the more we knew about everything—the easier it would be later on.

ERNESTINE [*thoughtfully*]. Of course.

FRANK [*thinking about it as he speaks*]. We'd be able to take care of ourselves better. There'd be less of a load on Mother.

ERNESTINE [*contritely*]. You can't blame him for not wanting us to waste time on dates and things like that, but—we didn't know.

FRANK. And he didn't know, either. I mean, like Mother said—about high school girls.

ERNESTINE. I guess boys—and things—Dad must have figured it was a shocking waste of time.

FRANK. The way I remember—the first boy to call—he came on the same night Dad had the big session with Doc Burton.

ERNESTINE. I think Dad and the doctor went upstairs after dinner that night. [*The stage lights come slowly up as the spotlight fades out on them.*]

FRANK [*as he and* ERNESTINE *move into room*]. That's right. You and I were over there playing checkers when they came down.

ERNESTINE. And I was wishing the phone would ring, and it would be some fullback who was dying to meet me. I didn't pay much attention to the checkers—or even to Dad. [*They move toward table* L C, *where a checkerboard has been set up. Mother's chair at* C *stage is* D L *again.*]

FRANK. Somehow you should realize right then. I mean, what the doctor was saying to Dad. You should understand at the time.

ERNESTINE. But at the time they seemed so casual. It just passed like any other conversation—like any ordinary conversation might pass.

FRANK [*indicating chair left of table*]. You were sitting there, and I was sitting here. [*They take their places.*]

ERNESTINE. And we hardly noticed. I guess I was day-dreaming. [*Puts her right elbow on table, rests her chin in palm, and looks off. The lights on the stage are now completely up.*]

FRANK. Hey, Ern! Your move.

ERNESTINE [*starting*]. What?

FRANK. Your move.

ERNESTINE [*regarding board reluctantly*]. Oh. [*Moves a piece.*]

FRANK [*inspecting move*]. Sure about that?

ERNESTINE [*irritated*]. Of course I'm sure.

FRANK [*shrugging*]. Okay. [*Takes one of his pieces and methodically jumps about six of* ERNESTINE'S *pieces.*]

ERNESTINE [*when she sees what he has done*]. I suppose you feel proud of yourself?

FRANK. Another game? [ERNESTINE *shrugs agreement.*]

[DAD *and* DR. BURTON *start down the stairs.* FRANK *and* ERNES-
TINE *are busy setting up the checkerboard for another game,
and pay no attention to* DAD *and the* DOCTOR.]

DAD [*with good humor*]. Quacks! You're all quacks!

DOCTOR. I hear it so much, there must be something to it.

DAD. The Gilbreths are rugged pioneer stock—no time for nonsense like being sick.

DOCTOR. What about the Gilbreth measles epidemic last spring?
[*Comes to sofa with* DAD.]

DAD. Probably even pioneers got the measles.

DOCTOR. It's possible.

DAD. You old fake—now you're trying to say I shouldn't take out
any three-year magazine subscriptions.

DOCTOR [*lightly*]. Absolute waste of money.

DAD [*slightly more serious*]. How about a one-year subscription?

DOCTOR. I'd still save my money. If I were you, I'd ask about
short-term subscriptions—maybe six months.

DAD [*after a momentary pause*]. That's a mighty short-term subscription.

DOCTOR [*dead serious for an instant*]. A man with your responsibilities doesn't want to waste his money. [*For a moment
they look at each other with full understanding. Then* DAD
brightens.]

DAD [*humorously*]. Mistah Bones—I don't believe a word you
say. I feel too good. Besides, I'm too busy.

DOCTOR [*smiling*]. Fine! Then I won't have to worry about
it. See you next week. [*Crosses to door* L.]

DAD [*after him*]. You bet you will. [DOCTOR BURTON *laughs and
goes out* L. FRANK *looks up from checker game.*]

FRANK. What magazine are you subscribing for, Dad?

DAD [*at door* L]. Never you mind. [*Notices checkers.*] What's
this? [*Pauses back of* ERNESTINE'S *chair.*]

ERNESTINE. We already did our homework.

DAD. That's fine, but you don't have to stop there. If you always
do more, pretty soon you skip a grade.

FRANK [*with a touch of indignation*]. But I just skipped a grade last year.

DAD. Start thinking about next year. I don't want you held back by a school system geared for the children of average parents. [*Crosses towards stairs.*] That's one of the topics for discussion tonight.

[ANNE *has started down the stairs. She holds up her skirt slightly before her as she comes.* MARTHA *is behind her.* ANNE *carries her manicure set.* MARTHA *has a book.*]

DAD [*noticing silk stockings, shaking his head in horror*]. Silk stockings!

ANNE [*nervously, pausing on landing, defending what she feels is right*]. I've been wearing them at school and I guess you might as well know it.

DAD [*somewhat heavily, again shaking his head*]. The next thing I know you'll be wanting to paint yourself.

ERNESTINE [*eagerly*]. Everybody uses make-up nowadays.

MARTHA. They don't call it painting any more.

DAD [*his voice rising with good-humored indignation*]. I don't care what they call it. I'll not have any painted women in this house! [*Starts up the stairs.*]

ANNE [*crossing to sofa*]. What you want is a house full of old maids!

DAD [*stopping on stairs, speaking seriously*]. What I want is for you to get ahead with things that matter—by yourselves—without needing me to hound you all the time.

ERNESTINE [*informing them*]. And the topic for tonight's family council is skipping grades at school.

DAD. Yes, by jingo, and a little better organization around here.

ANNE. We voted all topics should be of general interest.

DAD. Better organization is always of general interest. [*He goes up the stairs and out on this line.*]

ANNE. Dad's so smart. [*Unhappily.*] Why can't he understand? [*Sits on sofa and does her nails.* MARTHA *sits beside her and opens book.*]

FRANK [*jibing*]. You poor thing.

ERNESTINE [*her irritation turning on* FRANK]. Your move.
[FRANK *moves a piece.* ERNESTINE *continues sweetly.*] Sure?

FRANK. Of course. [ERNESTINE, *with great satisfaction, jumps
a number of his pieces.*] Hey—wait a minute!

ERNESTINE [*with her biggest smile*]. Another game?

FRANK. No.

[*From upstairs,* DAD *shouts, "Get him out of here!"* DAN *and*
FRED *come rushing down the stairs carrying a very large dog
between them.*]

DAN. Of all the dumb dogs!

FRED. What do you expect for five dollars? [*He and* DAN *go out
L with dog.*]

[BILL *starts down the stairs.*]

BILL [*grimly*]. Up on Dad's bed again.

MARTHA [*despairingly*]. He's *always* on Dad's bed. He's crazy
about Dad!

BILL [*nodding, as he comes to* C]. The basement window—
across the coal bin—up the back stairs—Dad's bed!

ANNE. He was right about the dog. Now he'll think he's right
about everything.

ERNESTINE. Clothes, make-up, and everything.

FRANK [*to* BILL]. They're still hoping the boys will go mad over
them.

BILL [*incredulously*]. Over *them?* [FRANK *nods.*]

MARTHA. What's so ridiculous about that?

BILL. Nothing, only——

ANNE. Only what?

ERNESTINE. If you've anything to say——

BILL. I just wouldn't think you'd have that sort of effect on any-
body.

FRANK. And we've known you all our lives. [*Being fair.*] Of
course, some boy who didn't know you so well——

ANNE [*bitterly*]. Thanks for the compliment.

BILL [*trying to patch things*]. I think you're very good swim-
mers—and at tennis.

ERNESTINE. We don't care for your opinion.

MARTHA. Other boys don't feel like that about us.

ANNE [*to* BILL]. Do they?

BILL [*shrugging*]. I've never even heard the subject mentioned.

FRANK [*rising*]. If you want an honest, frank answer——
[*Takes a deep breath.*]

ERNESTINE [*cutting him off*]. We don't.

FRANK [*sitting again*]. All those silk stockings—what good
did they do?

ANNE. Some day you're going to be surprised. [*Points to telephone.*] Some day that phone's going to ring and it'll be——
[*She is cut off sharply by sudden ring of telephone.* ALL *turn
towards it.* ANNE *is fascinated.*] And—it'll—be——

FRANK [*waving this away, crossing toward desk*]. Somebody for
Dad. [*Picks up telephone.*] Hello? . . . What? . . . [*Surprised.*] You want to talk with *who?* . . . You're absolutely
sure? . . . You haven't got her mixed up with somebody else?

ERNESTINE. Who's it for?

FRANK [*into telephone*]. You don't mean Anne Gilbreth, the
one with the freckles? . . . [ANNE *springs up from sofa and
moves toward desk. Her mouth forms words, "For me?"*]
My gosh! Don't hang up, please—are you still there? . . .
[*Listens, then:*] Thank goodness—please don't hang up.

ANNE [*in horror*]. What are you saying?

FRANK [*holding telephone so the boy can hear, too*]. Hey, Anne,
imagine! A boy calling for you! Isn't that wonderful! Hurry
before he hangs up!

ANNE [*sputtering*]. Give me that phone! [*Grabs it from him.*]

FRANK. Imagine—for *you!*

ANNE [*covering mouthpiece, to* FRANK]. You snake in the
grass! [*Then she takes her hand from mouthpiece, and speaks
in a honeyed voice.*] Hello . . . [*Nods.*] Yes, this is Anne
Gilbreth. . . . Who? . . . [*She has a hard time taking her*

eyes from FRANK *and* BILL, *who are trying to smother their mirth.*] It's nice of you—to call.

MARTHA [*whispering*]. Go ahead—talk to him.

ERNESTINE. Say something.

ANNE [*hand over mouthpiece, indicating* FRANK *and* BILL *helplessly*]. I can't!

ERNESTINE [*taking* DAD'S *cane from stand by door* L]. I'll take care of them. [*Starts after* FRANK *and* BILL, *and they flee up the stairs,* FRANK *calling, "We were only kidding."*] I'll fracture your skulls. [BILL *yells, "Hey, Frank, she means it."*] You bet I mean it. [*Before* ERNESTINE *can reach them, they disappear at head of stairs. As the boys go,* ANNE *takes her hand from mouthpiece.*]

ANNE [*haltingly, into telephone*]. No—nothing's the matter. . . . Yes, this is a very good time to call—yes. . . . [*Listens a moment, then repeating without understanding.*] Where-have-I-been-all-your-life? . . . [*Takes a breath.*] Mostly I've been right here. . . .

MARTHA [*whispering*]. Kid him along. [*Crosses close to* ANNE, ERNESTINE *following.*]

ANNE [*answering his question*]. Of course I'd be glad to have a soda with you. . . . [*Pause.*] You mean—now? . . . At night?

MARTHA [*whispering anxiously*]. What about Dad?

ANNE [*startled*]. You're driving right over?

MARTHA. Anne!

ERNESTINE [*anxiously*]. You don't have permission.

ANNE [*taking plunge*]. That'll be fine! Give a little toot on your horn when you get here. . . . [*With a cheerful smile and trying to sound gay.*] Be seeing you. [*Hangs up and turns to other girls. Her smile fades to a very worried expression.*]

MARTHA. Who is it?

ANNE. Joe Scales.

MARTHA. Golly—the cheerleader! And a car, too!

ERNESTINE. He's a little undersized.

ANNE [*moving to* C]. What if he is? You can't expect to start with the captain of the football team. But maybe if some people begin taking us out, then maybe—other people—will, maybe. [*Finishes lamely.*]

MARTHA [*a great asset*]. He's got the best car at school. [*Crosses to* C, ERNESTINE *following.*] You should hear it backfire!

ERNESTINE. What'll you tell Dad?

ANNE. Sooner or later, he's got to realize.

ERNESTINE. Don't you think it's better if he just realizes a little at a time?

ANNE. I don't know when I'll get another chance. I bet there'll be a lot of people down at the drugstore—I bet there'll be almost everybody.

ERNESTINE. If Dad lets you go——

MARTHA. He might have a project.

ANNE. Don't you see—this is the start. Boys notice girls that other boys notice. [*Moves* D L *as she talks, and turns.*] I mean, pretty soon you begin getting popular, and then you meet someone you really want to meet.

ERNESTINE. And if *you* start having dates, Dad can't be so strict with us.

MARTHA. No.

ANNE. That's why it's so important. It's the start of everything, that's all.

[MOTHER *enters and starts down the stairs.*]

ANNE [*seeing her*]. Mother——

MOTHER [*coming down and pausing above table* L C]. Your father will be down in a minute. He has some things for the family council to take up.

ANNE [*moving to chair left of table* L C]. Mother—there was a phone call. A boy called me.

MOTHER. That's nice.

ANNE. I think he's a very well-brought-up boy.

MARTHA. And he's the cheerleader!

ANNE. He asked me to go have a soda with him at the drugstore.

MOTHER. When?

ANNE. Tonight. He said he'd come right over.

MARTHA. He has his own car. [*They watch* MOTHER *anxiously.*]

MOTHER. I don't think tonight's a very good night for it. I think some other night . . .

ANNE [*miserably*]. If I break the first date I ever had, there won't *be* any other night.

ERNESTINE. Please, Mother.

MARTHA. Say something to Dad.

MOTHER. I wish—some other time. . . .

ANNE. But when—when?

MOTHER [*thoughtfully*]. I suppose you have to start sometime, though.

ANNE. I already told him "yes."

MOTHER [*after a pause*]. Maybe we could bring it up at the end of the council—if you'll be especially coöperative. I hope this boy is the quiet and reassuring type.

ANNE. Oh, he is!

ERNESTINE. He's small, too. Only that high! [*Indicates.*]

MOTHER [*starting toward door* R]. Well, that's reassuring.

[FRANK *and* BILL *come down the stairs.*]

BILL [*dashing down and waving an umbrella at* ERNESTINE]. Now we'll see whose skull gets fractured.

MOTHER. Bill, put down that umbrella. [BILL *lowers it, crestfallen, and continues on down the stairs.*]

[DAD *enters on stairs, gives his whistle, and starts down the stairs. Everyone moves at once.* LILLIAN *and* JACKIE *hurry in* R. DAD *crosses to the door* L, *whistles to outside, and then returns to* C *stage.*]

DAD. Frank—get a chair for your mother. [FRANK *scurries to* D L, *takes chair* D L, *and place. it at* C *stage.*]

[DAN *and* FRED *dash in* L. ALL *sit in the exact positions as in the previous council meeting.*]

DAN [*as his excuse*]. I was trying to explain things to the dog.

FRED. We made a new bed for him under the porch. He's sure to stay there.

DAD [*taking his position behind table* L C]. By jingo, he'd better! [*Raps on table with vase.*] I'm calling this meeting to order. If there are any topics of general interest you'd like to bring up—hearing none——

LILLIAN. Mr. Chairman, I'd like to go into the topic of roller-skates.

DAD. Not of general interest.

JACKIE [*standing up*]. I'm interested.

DAD. Sit down. [JACKIE *sits again.*]

DAN. The trouble is, you always decide what's of general interest, and none of us have a chance. I don't think that's very democratic.

DAD. Nonsense! I always favor a family discussion of general interest before going into the business of the meeting. [*Loftily.*] And I can't recall ever being unreasonable as to subject matter.

ANNE [*swallowing*]. I might sometime see a boy who's in my history class.

MARTHA. He's the cheerleader.

DAD. Not of general interest.

ERNESTINE. He is. We're all very interested. [GIRLS *nod emphatically.*]

DAD. Not me. I'm bored stiff. Now, if Anne had said she might sometime see a two-headed boy, that would be of general interest.

LILLIAN [*agreeing*]. I'd be very interested in a two-headed boy.

DAD. Now, *I* have a really first-rate topic. I want to teach you a new method of multiplication that's bound to make a wonderful impression on your math teachers. Remember, a lot of little things like this add up to skipping grades in school.

JACKIE. Is that of general interest, Daddy?

DAD. That, son, is a matter of the utmost general interest. Before we get into the mathematics, I'd like to make an announcement. I've been invited to speak at the World Management

Conference in London, and despite the opposition of a few worriers, I intend to go. But, by jingo, I'm going to leave this family in smooth-running condition—without a big load on your mother.

MOTHER. They're not such a load.

DAD. We're going to organize a purchasing committee to buy food, clothes, and equipment. Then I want you to elect a utilities officer to levy five-cent fines on wasters of water and electricity. A projects committee will see all work is completed on schedule. Your mother has enough to do as it is.

ANNE. We'll all help—of course, Dad. [*A general murmur of agreement comes from* CHILDREN.] And since that's settled—[*Nervously.*]—I move we adjourn.

DAD [*proceeding*]. We need more system. I'm installing work charts in the bathrooms, and you're to initial them every day after brushing teeth, bathing, doing homework, and so forth. Then your mother just has to glance at the charts.

ANNE. I think we're all in favor. [*Becoming nervous.*] And I think we ought to adjourn.

ERNESTINE. It's getting late.

MARTHA. It sure is.

DAD [*enthusiastically, continuing*]. I'd like to see us have the most efficient household in the whole world. That would leave more time for your studies. The *most* important thing is your schoolwork—your education.

ANNE. Couldn't we go into that tomorrow? We're all doing fine in our studies.

DAD. I want you doing better—skipping grades now and then. I don't want *anything* to interfere with your studies. [*The roar of an extremely noisy, backfiring, rattletrap car is heard, off* L, *coming closer.*]

ANNE [*jumping nervously*]. Mr. Chairman—please—I move we adjourn.

ERNESTINE. I second the motion.

DAD [*ignoring them*]. Your main job is getting ahead in school as fast as you can, and anything that detracts from that——

[*The car is now just outside door, and the noise is consider-able.*] And anything that detracts from that——[*A loud honking begins from car's horn.*] What I was trying to say ——[*Honking becomes more insistent. The* GIRLS *are in agony.*] Your schoolwork——[DAD *is cut short by* JOE'S *voice from off* L.]

JOE [*off* L]. Ann—eee! [*A burst of honks.*] Hey, Anneee! [ALL *turn and look at* ANNE.]

DAD [*to* ANNE, *grimly*]. Are you in any way responsible for that noise?

ANNE [*nodding weakly*]. I'm responsible. [*There is another burst of insistent honking.* ANNE *shuts her eyes in pain.*]

DAD [*looking out window*]. Great Caesar's ghost! [*Peering.*] What's that written on the car? [*Squints, as he reads it sober-ly.*] "Jump in, sardine. Here's your tin."

MARTHA. There's more on the other side.

MOTHER [*as* DAD *comes to* C *stage*]. He asked Anne if she could go have a soda with him. I think it might be all right.

ANNE. I've already done my homework.

DAD. We have a mathematics project.

ANNE. Couldn't I get it from Ernestine later? I promise I'll—— [*She is cut off by another burst of honking.*]

DAD [*irritated*]. Tell him to stop that.

ANNE [*rushing to door* L, *opening it, and calling*]. Joe—park the car and come in. [*Turns.*] Dad—oh, please——

MOTHER [*firmly, to* DAD]. Frank—I won't have you embarrass Anne.

DAD. What do you want me to do—go sit in the kitchen?

MOTHER [*pulling* DAD *towards the door* R]. We're going to have a talk before you say anything to that boy—he may be very nice.

MARTHA [*as if nothing more could be said*]. He's the cheer-leader!

DAD. That settles it.

MOTHER. Frank—you keep an open mind.

DAD [*as he goes out* R]. Anyone would think boys were more important than mathematics projects. [*He and* MOTHER *go out* R.]

MARTHA. Now what?

[ANNE *shrugs her bewilderment as* JOE SCALES *enters* L. *He is very short, and wears a bright, horizontally-striped sweater, loud pants, a bow tie, and pork-pie hat.*]

JOE. Hey—the gang's all here. [*To* ANNE.] What's the matter? Didn't you hear me honk? [ANNE *nods.*]

ERNESTINE [*softly*]. We heard you.

JOE [*proudly, pausing* D L *with* ANNE]. Some horn, hey?

ANNE [*indicating*]. My brothers—and sisters.

FRED. The babies are upstairs.

JOE. Some family!

DAN. You're the first cheerleader we ever saw up close.

JACKIE [*admiring*]. Gee!

JOE. How do you like my tie? That's a William Tell tie. [*Demonstrates by pulling tie away from his throat by elastic band and letting it snap back.*] You pull the bow—and it hits the apple—see? A William Tell tie. [*Repeats business.*] Pull the bow and it hits the apple! Some tie, hey? [*There is general reaction of admiration.* JOE *turns to* ANNE.] Say—we're running late. We better shove off.

ANNE. I think maybe my dad wants to meet you first.

ERNESTINE [*agreeing*]. I think maybe he will.

JOE. The gang's all down there. We ought to get going.

FRANK. Have you got time to show us how you lead a cheer?

JACKIE. Yes!

ANNE. No.

LILLIAN. Show us a cheer!

DAN. I'd like to see that!

JOE. Sure thing!

ANNE [*anxiously*]. Not now! Are you crazy?

JOE. I'll show you one cheer. Then we'll get going. **Okay?** [*Answering himself.*] Okay.

ANNE [*helplessly, pleading*]. No, no—don't!

JOE. What are you worrying about? [*Bounds over to* C *stage.*]
Come on and follow me. [*Cups his hands over his mouth and
shouts in a cracking baritone.*] Let's have a hoo, rah, ray, and
a tiger for Montclair High. A hoo, rah, ray, and a tiger. I want
to hear you holler now. Ready?

[DAD *pushes in* R, *followed by* MOTHER. ANNE *turns away in
horror.* JOE *drops on one knee and makes his fists go in a fast
circle.*]

JOE [*screaming*]. Hoo! [*The* GIRLS *are gesturing to* JOE, *warningly. He continues at top of his voice.*] Rah! [*Notes their
motions, his voice falling to almost nothing as he rises and
turns toward* DAD *and* MOTHER, *who have come* D R.]—Ray.

MOTHER [*to* DAD]. Now, Frank——

ANNE [*introducing* JOE]. Dad—I'd like you to meet Mr. Joe
Scales.

DAD [*civilly*]. How-do-you-do, young man?

JOE [*with a wide gesture*]. Hi, Pop. [DAD *starts.*]

MOTHER [*tugging* DAD'S *sleeve, in a calming voice*]. Remember
—now——

ANNE. Dad, Joe asked me to go have a soda with him. He says
all the gang's down at the drugstore.

DAD. How about the project?

ANNE [*since it means a lot*]. I'd like to go, Dad.

DAD [*regarding* ANNE *for a moment, realizing it really matters
to her*]. I'm always reasonable. A soda shouldn't take long.

ANNE [*joyously*]. You mean I can go?

DAD [*with a magnanimous gesture*]. Sure you can, honey!

ANNE [*overwhelmed, rushing to him,* D R, *throwing her arms
about him*]. Oh, Dad!

DAD [*glancing at watch*]. Let's see, now—I can take time out for
fifteen minutes—maybe twenty.

ANNE. Take time for what?

DAD. Chaperone you, of course.

JOE [*outraged*]. A chaperone! With me!

DAD [*turning to* JOE]. You didn't think I was letting her out of the house alone with you?

JOE [*indignantly*]. What's wrong with me?

DAD. It'd take more than fifteen minutes to answer that one.

JOE [*pointing off* L]. I can't walk into the drugstore—right in front of *everybody*—followed by a girl's father.

DAD [*imitating* JOE, *as he crosses to him at* C *stage*]. What's wrong with me?

MOTHER [*with twinkle*]. Young man—that's what they call a rhetorical question.

JOE. I don't care if it is. I'm not going to be chaperoned in any drugstore.

ANNE [*trying to calm him, crossing to* JOE *and* DAD *at* C *stage*]. Please—Joe.

JOE [*to* DAD]. Don't you trust your own flesh and blood.

MOTHER [*moving to right end of sofa*]. Of course he does.

DAD. Certainly I trust Anne. I trust all my children. [*Peers straight at* JOE.] It's cheerleaders I don't trust.

JOE. If that's the way you feel, I'm leaving. I'll get someone else. [*Moves to door* L.]

DAD. A judicious decision.

ANNE [*pleadingly, hurrying after him*]. Just a minute, Joe.

JOE [*scratching his head in wonder*]. I must have been crazy.

FRANK. Some date, hey?

JOE. Wait'll I tell the guys at the drugstore what happens when you date a Gilbreth.

ANNE [*horrified*]. You're not going to *tell* everyone?

ERNESTINE [*to* JOE]. It isn't Anne's fault!

JOE. Wait'll they hear. You'll get no more dates like me.

DAD. A hoo, ray, and a tiger for us.

JOE [*bewildered*]. Huh? [*Shaking his head, he goes out* L.]

ANNE [*in horror*]. Dad! [*Turns and opens door* L, *calling out.*] Joe—wait till I talk to you. [*The answer is the slam of a car door. Crushed,* ANNE *turns back into room. There is a pause.*] I can't see what harm would have been done if I'd gone for a soda. He'll tell them all. [*Miserably.*] I'm so embarrassed.

DAD. Cheerleaders! Absolute waste of time. [*Tries to whip up a little enthusiasm.*] Let's just do a *little* on the mathematics project. Then I'll take you all to the movies! We'll get a lot of candy and popcorn, and have a wonderful time! [*Looks at* ANNE *hopefully.*]

ANNE [*unhappily, moving slowly to her chair* D R *and sitting*]. Nobody in this family understands me. I wish I were dead.

DAD [*looking at her for a moment, and then speaking gently*]. What a thing to wish. [*Then, turning to others, he speaks forcefully.*] That's enough wasted time! I'm going to teach you how to multiply two-digit numbers in your head. [*The sound of* JOE'S *car bursting into life is heard.* ANNE *catches her breath, and, biting a knuckle, unhappily looks in direction of the sound.* DAD *firmly proceeds over sound of Joe's car as he drives off.*] The first example—to multiply forty-six times forty-six—you figure how much more forty-six is than twenty-five.

ANNE [*softly, miserably*]. There he goes. [*The curtain starts down.* ANNE *is still following sound of Joe's car.* MOTHER, *still standing by right end of sofa, looks over at* ANNE *with understanding.*]

DAD [*at* C *stage*]. Then you find how much less forty-six is than fifty—the answer is four—you square the four and get sixteen. [*But by now the curtain is down.*]

CURTAIN

ACT TWO

[*The houselights fade out. Music is heard playing. It is a jazzy old tune that comes on till it is almost blaring. Then it diminishes quickly until it is barely heard. The dim spotlight opens up at* D R *stage, again revealing* FRANK *and* ERNESTINE *standing in the same positions.*]

ERNESTINE [*turning to* FRANK *as music fades*]. They must have shut the window.

FRANK. Remember when the neighborhood Victrolas used to play that?

ERNESTINE [*nodding*]. And "Clap Hands, Here Comes Charlie," "Stumblin'," "Me and the Boy-friend."

FRANK [*smiling*]. "You Gotta See Mama Every Night or You Can't See Mama at All."

ERNESTINE. Those tunes make me think of a cheerleader back at Montclair High. [*Trying to remember.*] I can't recollect his name.

FRANK. Joe Scales. [*Turns sideways, striking a pose.*] Some sheik, hey?

ERNESTINE. Flaming youth had really caught fire—[*Ruefully.*] —except at our house.

FRANK [*agreeing*]. At our house, there was Dad.

ERNESTINE. And he acted as though he thought our generation was riding straight for the devil.

FRANK. In a stripped-down Model T, suitably inscribed with "Chicken, here's your roost—Four wheels, no brakes—The tin you love to touch."

ERNESTINE [*defensively*]. Those old jalopies were just as good as our own car.

FRANK [*smiling*]. Remember riding with Dad in the Pierce Arrow? Someone would call, "I see twelve kids!" Dad would bellow back—[*Imitates jovial Dad.*]—"These aren't much. You ought to see the ones I left home!" Once, someone shouted, "What you doing in that old ark?" And Dad shouted back, "I'm out collecting animals like the good Lord told me. All I need now is a jackass. Hop in!"

ERNESTINE. The most embarrassing part was when we'd come to a toll bridge, and Dad played his favorite game. He'd guess the nationality of the collector, then: "Hey, do my Irishmen come cheaper by the dozen?"

FRANK [*with a brogue*]. "Irishmen, is it! Sure and it wasn't meant for a family like that to pay toll."

ERNESTINE. Sometimes it was a Dutch collector.

FRANK [*imitating one*]. "Ach! What a fine lot of healthy Dutchmen! [*Gestures.*] Drive through on the house."

ERNESTINE. Even out for a drive, he couldn't stop teaching. I mean, if we passed a factory, he'd explain how they used a plumb-line to get the chimney straight.

FRANK. Because he was in a hurry for us. All the systems, study projects, committees——[*Jokingly.*] Were you terrible as head of the purchasing committee!

ERNESTINE [*stung*]. The purchasing committee got wholesale rates from underwear to baseballs. And look at the saving on canned food when we ordered direct by the truckload!

FRANK. How about the ninety-six jars of peanut butter?

ERNESTINE. Everybody likes lots of peanut butter.

FRANK. Not me. Not any more.

ERNESTINE. The committees were a wonderful idea. They eliminated waste motions, and made things easier for Mother.

FRANK. You didn't talk that way back then. Back then, all you girls thought about were boys and dates.

ERNESTINE. Because a boy hardly dared call at our house. That little cheerleader did everything but nail a quarantine sign on our door.

FRANK. I remember Anne burning up. [*Imitates her, dramatically with gestures.*] "I'm living through what can only be described as hell on earth!"

ERNESTINE. And Dad picked that particular time to step up the efficiency program.

FRANK [*after a slight pause*]. He didn't exactly "pick" that time.

ERNESTINE [*contritely, after a pause*]. I—didn't mean——

FRANK [*cutting in quickly*]. Sure. None of us knew. A lot of times it just seemed like he was extra impatient.

ERNESTINE. Like the time the lady psychologist came to give us those examinations.

FRANK. We didn't know about those exams. We didn't know they might mean Anne could graduate ahead of her class.

ERNESTINE. Dad's master plan. He was so anxious for Anne to get through school right then—so she could be free to help Mother.

FRANK [*trying to recollect*]. Didn't Anne go to a movie with some boy that afternoon?

ERNESTINE. She didn't know the exams meant anything. She didn't know Dad had been talking to the people at school about graduating her early.

FRANK [*remembering*]. But she missed dinner completely, and most of the tests. Dad was wild.

ERNESTINE. He kept checking his watch every three minutes. If the psychology teacher hadn't been there he'd have been roaring like a lion. [*The curtain begins to rise slowly on the darkened stage. The music gradually becomes louder.*]

FRANK. You and I finished the exam early—so did some of the others. I guess they'd gone upstairs. [*The music is louder. The lights on the stage come up gradually, as the spotlight fades out on* FRANK *and* ERNESTINE.]

ERNESTINE [*turning*]. Frank—that music—it isn't coming from down the street. That's one of our Victrolas—that's upstairs!

FRANK [*startled*]. The one in the girls' bathroom. [*Another Victrola comes on with a different tune. It plays simultaneously with the other.*]

ERNESTINE. The boys'!

FRANK [*apprehensively*]. Of all the dumb——

ERNESTINE. Dad's mad enough as it is.

FRANK. Boiling! We'd better switch them off. [*They move to-ward stairs.*]

ERNESTINE. Before Dad——

[ERNESTINE *is cut off by the sight of* DAD *hurrying in* R.]

DAD. Quiet! Shut off that *noise!* I said—*quiet!* [*One of the Victrolas is snapped off. He bellows.*] You, too! [*Other Victrola is snapped off. He comes to* FRANK *and* ERNESTINE.] Who's playing those?

ERNESTINE. I don't know. [FRANK *shrugs.*]

DAD. Anne didn't come in? [*Looks at* ERNESTINE. *She shakes her head. He look to* FRANK, *who also shakes his head.* DAD *takes out his watch and glares at it. From upstairs, a new sound comes from one of the Victrolas.*]

VICTROLA VOICE [*upstairs*]. Was ist das? Das ist der Ball. [DAD *looks up the stairs.*] Ist das der Ball? Ja, das ist der Ball.

FRANK. The boys' bathroom. [*Other Victrola comes on now, speaking French simultaneously with the German Victrola.*]

FIRST VICTROLA VOICE [*continuing, upstairs*]. Wie ist der Ball? Der Ball ist rund. Ist der Ball rund? Ja, der Ball ist rund. Ist der Ball schwarz? Ja, der Ball ist schwarz.

SECOND VICTROLA VOICE [*simultaneously, upstairs*]. Bonjour, mon ami. Quel est le nom de votre ami? Son nom est Gaston. J'ouvre la porte. Je ferme la porte.

ERNESTINE [*as second Victrola starts*]. The girls'.

DAD [*roaring, going up the stairs*]. No use trying to get around me now. Turn them off and come down here. Turn them *off!* [*Both Victrolas snap off.* DAD *turns to* FRANK *and* ERNESTINE, *with an apprehensive look* R.] That psychology teacher will think *I* told them to turn on those language lessons. She'll think I'm trying to impress her.

ERNESTINE. Well, aren't you? [*Moves down to sofa.*]

DAD [*scowling at her*]. How did you do on her trick examination?

ERNESTINE [*shrugging*]. Practically perfect.

FRANK [*modestly*]. Me, too. [*Joins* ERNESTINE *by sofa.*]

DAD [*crossing toward them*]. It didn't take you long to finish. [*Glares upstairs.*] You and whoever turned on those records.

[FRED *enters on the stairs.*]

FRED. Guten Abend.

[MARTHA *enters behind* FRED *on the stairs.*]

MARTHA [*with a grand gesture*]. Bonsoir, mon père.

DAD. If you spent half as much time improving your minds as you do memorizing those stupid songs, you could recite the "Koran" forwards and backwards.

FRED [*dramatically, on landing*]. Ich bin durstig—Die Milch ist gut. Das Wasser ist kalt. Ich muss ein Apfel haben.

MARTHA [*reciting, with gestures, and joining* FRED *on landing*]. Frère Jacques. Frère Jacques. Dormez-vous—dormez-vous.

FRED [*joining in*]. Ich weis nicht was soll es bedeuten, das ich so traurig bin——

MARTHA [*simultaneously with* FRED]. Sonnez les matines—sonnez les matines——

FRED [*at the same time as* MARTHA]. Ein Märchen aus alten Zeiten, das kommt mir nicht aus dem Sinn.

MARTHA. Ding-dong-bell—ding-dong bell!

DAD [*with great sarcasm*]. No. Let's wind up the Victrola and have more jazz. [*Sings in an exaggerated style.*] Da-da, de-da-da. Let's have that record about "I'll Love My Sweetie Forever and a Day."

FRED [*coming down to left of table* L C]. You made it up. That's not a record.

DAD. Maybe not. But take it from me, that's well above average. Da-da, de-da-da——

MARTHA [*coming above table* L C]. We bought those jazz records with our own money—Anne, Ern, and me. [*Shrugs.*] Who wants to recite the "Koran" backwards.

DAD [*indignantly*]. Look at the report cards you brought home this afternoon!

ERNESTINE. What's so wrong with a "B" average?

DAD. Last year you got straight "A's."

ERNESTINE. Last year I skipped a grade. It takes a while to catch up.

DAD. Just the same—these afternoons in the drugstore with the boys—drinking sodas and listening to jazz. I told you it wouldn't help your marks, and this proves I was right.

ERNESTINE. We hardly spend *any* time with boys.

FRANK [*sprawled out on sofa*]. Ha!

MARTHA. We don't have what some people would call a normal social life. Some people have dates on school nights.

DAD [*glaring at watch again as he paces* D R]. It's practically night now, and a school night, and where's your sister?

MARTHA. We told you ten times.

ERNESTINE [*in singsong voice*]. She-went-to-a-movie-with-a-boy.

DAD. *All* afternoon? She missed dinner! She's missing the examination! She *knows* she should be home!

FRED. Bill went with her.

ERNESTINE. She remembered your rule—a brother on every date.

DAD. But she's making him miss the test, too. [*Angrily, moving to right end of sofa.*] Why didn't she just bring this boy to the house instead of going off like that?

MARTHA [*throwing her hands up*]. Why?

DAD. Yes, why?

ERNESTINE. Because of the way you scared Joe Scales. He's got the rest of the boys afraid to come here. Even that friend of mine.

DAD [*disapprovingly*]. The one with the motorcycle? [ERNESTINE *nods enthusiastically.*] The one who keeps buzzing the house with that noise contraption? At all hours?

ERNESTINE [*defensively*]. He's trying to work up nerve to come in.

DAD [*sharply*]. What's he afraid of?

ERNESTINE. You.

DAD. Me! Why should any boy be afraid of *me!* [*Sound of a*

*motorcycle heard in the distance. Sound rapidly gets **nearer**
and louder.*]

ERNESTINE [*raptly*]. It's—I think it's Mac!

DAD. Run out and tell him your father's leaving soon for the
Management Conference in Europe. Tell him he won't have
to work on his nerve much longer.

MARTHA. She already told him. [ERNESTINE *nods "yes." Sound
of motorcycle pauses outside door* L.]

ERNESTINE [*enraptured*]. He's stopping! Maybe he'll come in!
[*Then sound roars up again and goes off into distance.* ER-
NESTINE *is disappointed.*] There he goes.

MARTHA. Joe Scales' car is much louder.

[MOTHER *enters* R.]

MOTHER. I hear "Motorcycle Mac." [*Comes down to* DAD.]

DAD. He's still working on his nerve.

[MRS. FITZGERALD *enters* R.]

MOTHER. Is Anne back yet?

DAD. No. [*Strides over toward door* L.] For all I know, she
eloped.

ERNESTINE [*indignantly*]. She-went-to-a-*movie!*

MRS. FITZGERALD. Mrs. Gilbreth—I'm not getting any help in
the kitchen.

MOTHER. With all these examinations, things are upset.

DAD [*to* CHILDREN]. Hop to it.

MOTHER. Mart and Ern better see to the babies. [MARTHA *and*
ERNESTINE *nod and start up the stairs.*]

FRANK [*reluctantly*]. I'm not supposed to wash dishes. [*Rises
reluctantly.*]

FRED. What about Dan and Jackie and Lillian, too?

MOTHER. They're finishing the exam.

FRED [*as he and* FRANK *cross* R]. Now I know why they're taking so long. [*Goes out* R *with* FRANK *as* MARTHA *and* ERNEST-
INE *go upstairs and out.*]

MRS. FITZGERALD [*pausing before returning to kitchen*]. I thought they were a scream at dinner.

DAD. Who? [*Comes to table* L C.]

MRS. FITZGERALD. With the woman examiner.

MOTHER [*with slight distaste*]. Miss Brill.

MRS. FITZGERALD [*greatly amused*]. She came late and was trying to catch up—Jackie tried to be so helpful. He told her: "No need to gobble your grapefruit like a pig. If we finish ahead of you, we'll wait till you're through."

DAD. They made a bad impression.

MRS. FITZGERALD. And Lillian——

MOTHER [*smiling*]. She thinks family rules apply to guests.

MRS. FITZGERALD [*making little gesture*]. "Sorry, but I'm afraid I can't pass your dessert till you finish your lima beans." [*Goes out* R, *chuckling to herself.*]

DAD [*thoughtfully*]. And it didn't help when Jackie asked if what Miss Brill was saying was of general interest.

MOTHER. As a matter of fact, I don't think they care for Miss Brill, and I don't, either. I don't think she's being fair. [*Sits on sofa.*]

DAD [*coming to* C]. Of all the fine teachers here, we had to get that one!

MOTHER. She asked all sorts of slanted questions, and I don't think she's marking the papers fairly.

DAD. Yes, and she's blocking my most important plan.

MOTHER. Plan? I thought this was just one of the school's research projects.

DAD. That, too.

MOTHER. Does this have something to do with all your trips to school?

DAD [*sitting in chair right of table* L C]. With Anne's record, it's ridiculous for her to have to mark time with her class. There's no reason why they shouldn't graduate her at the end of this semester.

MOTHER. That's going awfully fast. She skipped a grade last year.

DAD. But once she graduates she won't have to worry about schoolwork for a while. With me away, you could use a little help.

MOTHER. But Anne doesn't know this test will have any bearing on when she graduates.

DAD. I worked out an agreement with the superintendent. He's writing a paper on the effects of home education—and naturally he came to the right source for that.

MOTHER [*smiling*]. Naturally!

DAD. I told him he could have his Miss Brill snoop around all she wants. But in return, he's got to do something for me.

MOTHER. He's going to give Anne her diploma?

DAD. If her mark's good enough. [*Rises.*] And, by jingo, it better be. [*Glances at watch again.*] What's the matter with that girl!

[MISS BRILL *has entered* R *with several papers in her hand.*]

MISS BRILL [*coming down to right of sofa*]. I presume you're talking about your daughter Anne.

MOTHER [*rising*]. There's not a thing the matter with any of our children.

DAD. You'll find that out when you grade Anne's paper.

MISS BRILL. And when will that be?

DAD. Don't worry, she'll be here. She's the youngest girl in her class and always gets "A's."

MISS BRILL. Where did she go?

DAD [*irritably, imitating* ERNESTINE'S *singsong voice*]. She-went-to-a-movie! [*Paces to door* L.]

MISS BRILL. These examinations are a little more important. [*In awe.*] They're for the superintendent!

DAD. I know who they're for, and they're important to me, too.

MISS BRILL. The superintendent directed me to give these tests. That doesn't mean I approve of anyone graduating ahead of her class. And if she doesn't show up, that's perfectly all right with me.

DAD [*quickly*]. She'll be back any minute.

MOTHER. What have you learned so far? About the others?

MISS BRILL. The results aren't conclusive.

DAD [*coming back to* C *stage*]. What's inconclusive about them? Did you ever grade a better set of papers?

MISS BRILL. I have to interpret the results.

DAD [*exploding*]. Interpret! Here's something to interpret! [*Takes out his stop-watch, whistles assembly call, and then clicks watch.*]

MISS BRILL [*startled*]. What's that?

MOTHER [*smiling*]. You'll see. [*Moves to* DAD.]

[LILLIAN, DAN, *and* JACKIE *dash in* R *and line up.* MARTHA *and* ERNESTINE *hurry down the stairs and take their positions.* FRANK *and* FRED *dash in* R. *They are both wearing aprons and have their sleeves rolled up. The line is completed, as before, with the exception of* ANNE *and* BILL. MISS BRILL *is startled by the sudden rush, and takes refuge* D R.]

CHILDREN [*as they assemble*]. Now what? I finished the test already. What is it? What's up, Dad? Did I pass? Here I am. Anything happen?

DAD [*as last one is in line, clicking watch and snapping up his head*]. Ten seconds.

DAN. Wow!

DAD. Doesn't count. Bill and your older sister aren't here.

DAN. Awww——

DAD. Frank—what's forty-six times forty-six

FRANK [*taking step forward*]. Twenty-one sixteen. [*Steps back.*]

DAD. Dan—nineteen times seventeen?

DAN [*repeating business*]. Three twenty-three.

DAD. Martha. Fifty-two times fifty-two?

MARTHA [*repeating business*]. Twenty-seven, zero, four.

DAD. Good girl! [*Casts a look at* MISS BRILL.]

MISS BRILL. You've coached them.

DAD. I *taught* them. [*Sharply.*] Do you know the capital of Columbia? Do you know the population of Des Moines according to the last census? Of course you do—but so does Dan here—so does Lillian—so does baby Jane upstairs. I'd bring her down, but it's time for her bottle.

MISS BRILL. Now you're being ridiculous.

DAD. What's sixteen times sixteen?

MISS BRILL. Well—I—really——

JACKIE. Two fifty-six.

DAD. There! What's seventeen times seventeen? [MISS BRILL *shakes her head.*]

JACKIE. Two eight-nine.

DAD [*a sigh of pleasure*]. Good, Jackie-boy. [*To* MOTHER.] Boss, we'd better keep that boy.

MOTHER [*to* MISS BRILL]. Are there some questions *you'd* like to ask?

DAD. To help you interpret?

MISS BRILL. I have all I need on these proper examinations.

DAD. No questions. [*To* CHILDREN.] Dismissed. Get on with things. Snap along now. [CHILDREN *break up.* LILLIAN, FRANK, *and* FRED *pile out* R. MARTHA *and* ERNESTINE *go upstairs, followed by* DAN.

MOTHER [*to* FRANK, *as he goes out* R]. Tell Mrs. Fitzgerald to keep some dinner warm.

FRANK. Sure!

MISS BRILL [*coming to sofa*]. There's no harm in home studies. But you shouldn't try to do so much with them.

DAD. Why not?

MISS BRILL. If everyone went in for irregular education like that, there wouldn't be any system left. There'd be chaos.

DAD. Perhaps you'd better mark the papers and see how much chaos you find.

MOTHER. You can use the dining-room table.

MISS BRILL [*starting* R]. Thank you.

MOTHER [*crossing after her*]. If you don't mind—I'll look over your shoulder.

MISS BRILL. I *do* mind. [*Goes out* R.]

MOTHER [*with mock shock*]. Miss Brill!

DAD [*starting* R]. The old goat.

MOTHER. Go up and lie down for a little. [*Takes his arm and starts toward stairs*]. Doctor Burton said you should lie down for a little after dinner.

DAD [*reluctantly being led upstairs*]. He's an old goat, too.

MOTHER. A little rest won't hurt you. [DAD *pauses on stairs, takes out his watch, checks time again, glances back into room, and then goes upstairs and out with* MOTHER. *There is a momentary pause. Then:*]

DAD [*offstage, upstairs, roaring*]. Get him out of here!

[DAN *and* JACKIE *come dashing down the stairs carrying the big dog between them.*]

DAN [*to dog*]. Won't you ever learn?

JACKIE [*angrily, to dog*]. Why always Dad's bed? Why not my bed, or Dan's bed, or Frank's bed, or Martha's bed, or Anne's bed? Why always *Dad's* bed?

DAN [*shrugging*]. He just attracts dogs. [*He and* JACKIE *go out* L *with dog.*]

[*For a moment, the stage is empty. Then the door* L *opens.* BILL *bursts in and moves to* C *stage. He acts very much put-out. Then* ANNE *enters* L, *turns back, and calls.*]

ANNE. Come on in, Larry.

[LARRY, *a nice-looking boy, enters* L *somewhat hesitantly.*]

ANNE [*smiling at him*]. Just— my house.

BILL. I'm starved.

ANNE [*irritably*]. Well, go eat.

BILL. Don't worry. And don't think I didn't notice.

ANNE. Notice what?

BILL. Remember that silly part in the movie? [*They nod.*] That part all about—[*With distaste.*]—love? [*Continues, accusingly.*] I saw you hold hands.

ANNE [*gasping*]. That's a lie! [BILL *folds his arms and glares.*]

LARRY. If anything like that happened, for maybe ten seconds, it was just because of the movie and entirely involuntary.

ANNE [*turning towards* LARRY, *wistfully*]. It was?

LARRY [*nodding*]. It was just that kind of a movie.

ANNE [*swallowing her disappointment*]. Oh.

BILL [*to* ANNE]. See?

ANNE [*bitterly, to* BILL, *crossing toward him*]. Having you tag along is simply unendurable.

BILL [*indignantly*]. I suppose you think it's durable to me? [*Shakes his head and crosses* R.] I'm starving to death. [*Goes out* R.]

LARRY [*with distaste*]. Kid brothers.

ANNE [*no false pretenses*]. In case you don't already know, I have six of them. [*Swallows.*] Six berserk kid brothers.

LARRY [*crossing to her*]. I already know.

ANNE [*relieved*]. Thank heaven.

LARRY. Say, I bet you're getting hungry.

ANNE [*—How could he say such a thing!*] Hungry!

LARRY. I made you miss dinner.

ANNE [*with scorn*]. I miss dinner all the time. [*Sits on sofa.*] I hate dinner—in fact, if there's one thing on earth I don't care if I miss—it's—dinner.

LARRY [*surprised at himself*]. I don't seem to be very hungry, either.

ANNE [*pleased*]. You're not?

LARRY. Of course, I ate an awful lot of popcorn.

ANNE [*nodding dolefully*]. And gumdrops.

LARRY [*still surprised at himself*]. Of course, that never interfered with my appetite before. Say, would you like to go to a dance?

ANNE [*taking a breath*]. I'd——[*Cuts herself short, then proceeds with studied casualness.*] I mean, I could probably fit it in—depending on when the dance is.

LARRY. Tonight—a bunch of the seniors.

ANNE. It just happens—tonight I'm free.

LARRY. Swell! I'll change and be back for you in half an hour. [*Starts* L *and then turns back.*] I'm glad your dad isn't old-fashioned about letting you go out on school nights.

ANNE [*rising, moving toward him*]. School night! Wait, Larry. [*With difficulty.*] There's someone I have to check with first.

LARRY. Some other boy?

ANNE [*with glance toward stairs*]. Well, he's male.

LARRY [*upset*]. I didn't think you were the kind that stalls a fellow while she sees if she can get a better date.

ANNE [*anxiously*]. I'm not! It's not that at all. Really, Larry, I'd love to go with you. But—I have to get through a short examination first—and, well—like I told you——

[BILL *enters* R, *chewing on a sandwich. They are not aware of him.*]

LARRY [*holding out his hands to her*]. Honestly?

ANNE [*nodding*]. Honestly. [*Takes his hands.*] But I'd rather go to a dance with you—than with—*anyone*.

LARRY [*mollified*]. That's different.

BILL [*who has been observing the hands, comes to right end of sofa*]. At it again! [*They jerk their hands apart, and separate further.* BILL *continues reproachfully.*] The minute my back is turned!

ANNE. You don't have to sneak up on people. You might cough —or something.

BILL [*waving sandwich*]. Just try coughing with your mouth full of peanut butter. [*Starts up the stairs.*] I have to tell Dad we're back.

ANNE [*crossing to foot of stairs*]. Bill—Mother said we were not to worry Dad with unimportant worries.

BILL. Who said I was going to worry him. [*Completes his exit up the stairs.*]

LARRY. I hope he doesn't get your father mad.

ANNE [*without conviction*]. He won't. [*Grimly, coming to* C.] He'd better not.

LARRY [*awkwardly, moving toward her*]. I heard about your father.

ANNE. Lots of people hear about Dad and his work.

LARRY. It wasn't exactly about—his work.

ANNE. The way he eliminates waste motion and things like that? [LARRY *shakes his head. She continues apprehensively.*] What'd you hear?

LARRY [*with a depreciating smile*]. Tell you the truth, I was almost afraid to come here.

ANNE [*emphasizing a surprise she doesn't feel*]. No?

LARRY [*nodding*]. I didn't know whether to ask you for a date or not.

ANNE [*laughing at the idea*]. You haven't been listening to that little cheerleader? That Joe Scales?

LARRY. How'd you know?

ANNE [*exclaiming*]. Really! [*Crosses to right end of sofa.*] The things that boy says about my father. Why, he'd say *anything!*

LARRY [*crossing down to her*]. He would?

ANNE. You'd think my dad was some kind of monster—when actually——

LARRY. Yes?

ANNE. He's friendly and agreeable and witty—and has one of the sweetest tempers—and——[*She is cut short by a roar from* DAD *offstage, upstairs.*]

DAD [*offstage, upstairs*]. So she's back, is she?

ANNE [*with a fearful glance toward stairs*]. And—those stories —just absurd!

LARRY. I'm glad to hear it.

DAD [*roaring, offstage*]. *What took her so long?*

ANNE [*gulping*]. He must be calling to someone—someone at the back of the house. [*Smiles.*] When Dad calls to the back of the house, you can also hear him at the front of the house.

LARRY [*with a glance toward stairs*]. I guess you can.

ANNE. No reason why you shouldn't come here.

DAD [*offstage*]. *You mean that boy's down there right now?*

MOTHER [*offstage, upstairs*]. Shush, Frank.

DAD [*offstage*]. *I won't shush!* [ANNE *bites her hand at this.*]

LARRY [*hesitantly*]. I guess I'd better be getting along.

ANNE [*defeated*]. I suppose you had.

LARRY [*with glance at stairs, then back to* ANNE]. Guess I'd better. [*Goes quickly to door* L.]

ANNE [*trying to repress her concern, moving after him*]. About the dance—I don't suppose—I mean——

LARRY. Yes?

ANNE. What I mean is—[*The question at last.*]—will you be coming back?

DAD [*angrily, offstage*]. B-y j-i-n-g-o! [ANNE *winces at this, shutting her eyes with pain.*]

ANNE [*opening her eyes, taking a breath*]. Will you?

LARRY [*squaring his shoulders*]. I asked you to the dance, didn't I? [*Gives one more uneasy glance toward stairs. Then:*] Well —be seeing you, then. [*Goes out* L *door, leaving the overwhelmed* ANNE. *She puts her hand to her mouth as though to hold back a cry of pleasure.*]

[D*r* ⁻ *starts down the stairs, followed by* MOTHER *and then* BILL *He stops at the sight of* ANNE.]

DAD [*pointing a finger at her*]. Look at her!

ANNE [*unable to contain her joy*]. I told you if I started dressing like other girls, everything would be all right, and I'd be popular.

DAD. Popular! Missing dinner—dodging tests——[*Outraged.*] By jingo, you've started painting yourself, too!

ANNE. I haven't!

DAD [*coming on down the stairs to* C *stage*]. I can see the paint! [*Stops short and takes several loud sniffs.*] Perfume! You've started using perfume!

MOTHER [*coming above table* L C]. Frank—she hasn't even had her dinner. [BILL *ambles over to sofa and sits on left arm.*]

DAD. It's her fault. [*With horror.*] Perfume!

ANNE. Just one dab. [*Defiant, crossing to* DAD *at* C *stage.*] Why not? It isn't painting or make-up, and it smells so good.

DAD. Why not? Because it stinks up good fresh air, that's why not. You're going to wash it off.

ANNE. Oh, Dad!

DAD. Do you know what men think when they smell perfume on a woman?

ANNE. I only know what one man thinks. He thinks I should wash it off.

DAD. Thinks—nothing! [*Points* R.] And you get in there and take that examination.

MOTHER. She's going to eat something first.

BILL. Me, too.

ANNE [*moving* D R]. I don't want to eat. I want to get the exam over with, first. [*Determined.*] I've something to do later.

DAD. Probably something to do with that boy.

ANNE [*bursting out*]. Why do I need a brother tagging along when I go to a movie with someone! It's intolerable. Really, I don't know why any boy bothers with me.

DAD. Well, I know, even if you don't. And that's why a brother goes along.

ANNE [*coming to right end of sofa*]. Supposing I wanted to go to a dance? A really important dance that just happens for instance to fall—[*Swallows.*]—on a school night.

MOTHER. Now—we can think about that when the time comes.

ANNE [*taking big breath*]. Mother—Dad——

DAD. No more nonsense, now. Out all this time, perfume, painting your face——

BILL [*echoing* DAD]. It's awful.

MOTHER [*disapprovingly, to* BILL]. You go along to the dining-room and report to Miss Brill. [BILL *goes out* R. *Sound of motorcycle is heard, coming closer and louder.*]

DAD. Anne——

MOTHER [*equally determined, crossing to him at* C *stage*]. Now, Frank!

DAD. All right, then—you handle it. [*Starts up the stairs, indignantly.*] Movies! Perfume! Painting! [*Pauses.*] Thank heaven my other daughters are a little more sensible—**not** quite so——

[MARTHA *and* ERNESTINE *rush down the stairs.* DAD'S *voice trails off.*]

DAD. Not quite so—silly.

ERNESTINE [*oblivious to all else*]. It's "Motorcycle Mac"!

MARTHA [*as they rush to window* U R C]. Maybe this time he'll stop.

DAD [*shaking head in horror*]. Oh! [*Goes upstairs and out.*]

ERNESTINE. No—he's going on. [*Sound of motorcycle continues, dying in distance.*]

MARTHA [*turning*]. Hi, Anne!

ERNESTINE. Where were you?

ANNE [*shaking her head at them, intently, crossing to* MOTHER.] Mother—I did put on one dab of perfume, but I *didn't* use any make-up at all—not any. [*Rubs handkerchief against her cheek and shows it to* MOTHER.] See?

MOTHER. I'll explain to Dad later.

ANNE. It's just—color.

MOTHER [*smiling*]. Your color's very good tonight.

ANNE [*hesitating*]. There's a reason. [*Then quickly.*] I'd like to get going on that exam.

ERNESTINE [*coming back of sofa, with* MARTHA]. Who'd you go with?

MARTHA. That fullback?

ANNE [*nodding*]. Larry. [*Turns to* MOTHER.] Mother—I had a *wonderful* afternoon!

MOTHER [*gently*]. You shouldn't have stayed so long. We worried about you. Especially your father.

ANNE. Why does Dad care so much? I mean, what if I do waste one afternoon?

MOTHER. Your father wants everything shipshape and efficient before he leaves for Europe. Besides, there's this test.

ANNE. Why'd they have to send that Miss Brill?

MOTHER. I'm sure she's a fine teacher, dear. [*Crosses* R.] I'll tell her you're here. [*Goes out* R.]

ERNESTINE [*hurrying to* ANNE, *followed by* MARTHA]. What's up?

MARTHA. What's going on?

ANNE [*breathlessly*]. Larry asked me to a dance. He's coming right back for me.

ERNESTINE. Are you crazy? It's a school night. What are you going to tell Dad?

ANNE. I don't know. I'd better get the exam out of the way, first. Is it tough?

ERNESTINE [*sitting on sofa*]. The same old I.Q. stuff. It's a snap.

MARTHA. Especially for Miss I.Q. of Montclair High.

ANNE [*wistfully*]. I wish I could be Miss Something Else.

ERNESTINE [*smiling*]. You're stuck with it.

MARTHA [*sitting on left arm of sofa*]. For once your I.Q. is going to be put to some good use. I can't wait to see Miss Brill's face when she grades your paper.

ERNESTINE. I have a feeling she's dying to bear down with that red pencil.

MARTHA. Even I didn't have much trouble with the written part.

ERNESTINE. And the word-association test—there's nothing to it.

MARTHA. She just shoots five words at you.

ANNE. Swell! [*Moves toward door* R.] I'm in an awful rush.

MARTHA [*savoring thought*]. If I told you the five words, you could really pour it on her, when she asks.

ANNE. Well, don't.

MARTHA. Golly, her mouth would just drop wide open.

ANNE. I'd better get in there. [*Pauses as* ERNESTINE *speaks*.]

ERNESTINE [*thinking about* MARTHA'S *suggestion*]. You know, if every time she popped a word at you and you could pop back a lot of answers, a whole string of associated words . . .

MARTHA [*to* ERNESTINE]. Of course it wouldn't be right if we told Anne the words in the test.

ANNE. No, it wouldn't, and I'd better get a move on. [*Starts to go, and pauses again.*]

MARTHA [*still to* ERNESTINE]. It would be wrong to tell her that the first word is "knife."

ANNE. Don't!

MARTHA [*ostentatiously, to* ERNESTINE]. Or that the second word is "black."

ANNE [*coming to right end of sofa*]. Please.

MARTHA [*quickly*]. "Foot, hair, bird."

ANNE [*bothered*]. You shouldn't have told me.

ERNESTINE. No, you certainly shouldn't have told her that the five words are—[*Enunciates clearly.*]—"knife, black, foot, hair, bird." You ought to be ashamed of yourself.

MARTHA. Gee, I'm sorry. [*With mock earnestness.*] Anne, put them out of your mind. Try to forget that the five words are "knife, black, foot, hair, bird."

ANNE. Forget them? After the way you've been drumming them in. [*Clutches head.*] Good night, I'm already thinking of the answers. Why did you do a thing like that!

[DAD *appears on the stairs, carrying some papers.*]

DAD [*to* ANNE]. Aren't you ever going to get down to business?

ANNE. Right now. [*Hurries out* R.]

DAD [*to* ERNESTINE *and* MARTHA, *coming to table* L C]. I thought your mother told you to see to the babies.

ERNESTINE. We were seeing to them. [*She and* MARTHA *start up the stairs.*]

DAD [*moving to sofa*]. Till a motorcycle passes the house.

MARTHA. I think motorcycles are wonderful. You can make a lot of noise with a motorcycle. [*She and* ERNESTINE *go upstairs and out.*]

[MOTHER *enters* R *as* DAD *sits on sofa and starts arranging the papers.*]

MOTHER [*coming behind sofa*]. Anne's just breezing through the test.

DAD. About time she did some breezing.

MOTHER. I think she has a crush on one of the boys at school.

DAD. Boss, here are the charts I've worked out—rotation of duties and assignments, records of results. I want to get all of this functioning before I leave.

MOTHER [*leaning over back of sofa*]. I wish you wouldn't go. Doctor Burton says——

DAD [*who has had enough of that already*]. Doctor Burton— Doctor Burton! We'd better concentrate on some way to knock a little sense into our older daughters.

MOTHER [*smiling*]. They're perfectly normal—at least they want to be.

DAD. They want to be wasting a lot of time. [*With a slight pause.*] And time's too precious.

MOTHER [*crossing around sofa and sitting next to him*]. Is it really so important to go to this Management Conference?

DAD [*seriously*]. A conference like that gives me a chance to explain motion study to the world. [*Wryly.*] The world could stand a little efficiency. Besides, it can be awfully good for business. It costs a lot to run a family like this.

MOTHER [*smiling*]. Remember when we first talked about the family we'd have? Our wedding day. You said we'd have a wonderful life and a wonderful family. A great big family.

DAD. I warned you—children from the basement to the attic; from the floorboards to the chandeliers.

MOTHER. And when we went for a Sunday walk, we'd look like Mr. and Mrs. Pied Piper.

DAD [*gravely*]. Mrs. Piper, shake hands with Mr. Piper. [*Takes her hands tenderly.*] Mr. Piper, meet Mrs. Piper.

MOTHER. I asked you how many children—just as an estimate. You told me—just as an estimate—many.

DAD. That day when we got on the train—you tried to appear so blasé—as if we'd been married for years.

MOTHER [*smiling in reprimand*]. And when I took off my hat, you gave that loud whisper—"Good lord, woman, why didn't

you tell me your hair was that color?" Everyone turned around
to leer and wink.

DAD. I shouldn't have done that. It was just that I was so proud
of you. I wanted everyone to look at you and know you were
my wife. [MOTHER *puts her hand on his arm.* DAD *goes back
to papers.*] I think the work charts and committees are working out fine. [*Pleased.*] The family's getting so it runs itself.

MOTHER. You've thought of most everything, Mr. Piper.

DAD. Thank you, Mrs. Piper.

[MISS BRILL *enters* R.]

DAD [*seeing her, rising, moving to table* L C, *putting down
papers*]. I told you Anne would be back in time.

MISS BRILL [*coming above sofa to* C *stage*]. I don't think she's
taking the test seriously. She's just marking answers down the
page as fast as she can go.

MOTHER. She said something about being in a hurry.

DAD. Mmm . . .

MISS BRILL [*sniffing*]. Perhaps she has something more important.

[ANNE *enters* R, *with a paper in her hand.*]

DAD. What is it?

MISS BRILL [*severely*]. You're not supposed to leave the table
till you're finished.

ANNE [*handing over her paper to* MISS BRILL *at* C *stage*]. I am
finished.

MISS BRILL. That's impossible!

ANNE [*with finality*]. It's finished.

DAD [*concerned*]. You answered all questions? The best you
could?

ANNE. Honestly, Dad, it was a snap.

MISS BRILL. A snap! [*Sits left of table* L C *and starts going down
paper with pencil.*] We'll see how much of a snap it is.

DAD [*folding arms confidently*]. You bet we'll see. [*A pause as
they watch* MISS BRILL *grade paper.*]

MISS BRILL [*her voice trailing off*]. We'll just see how much of
a . . . [*Pause.*] Hmmm . . . [*Marks another question.*]
Dear me.

DAD. What's the matter?

MISS BRILL [*swallowing*]. There doesn't seem to be *anything* the
matter.

DAD. You haven't found any wrong answers?

MISS BRILL. Not yet.

DAD. Keep marking.

MISS BRILL. I will. [*Another pause while she marks.*] My goodness!

DAD. Yet?

MISS BRILL [*grudgingly*]. Not yet.

DAD [*beaming*]. Just keep on marking. [MISS BRILL *marks several more questions and then pushes paper aside.*]

MISS BRILL. I can't properly mark a paper under conditions like
these.

DAD [*with a smug smile*]. Yet?

MISS BRILL [*burning up*]. No, not yet.

DAD. Good girl, Anne. [*Turns to* MOTHER.] By jingo, we'll tell
the whole family about this. [*Whistles assembly call enthusiastically and speaks proudly.*] She's a chip off the old block.
[MOTHER *rises and joins* DAD.]

[*The* CHILDREN *dash in:* MARTHA *and* ERNESTINE *down the
stairs;* BILL, FRANK, FRED, *and* LILLIAN *from* R; JACKIE *and
DAN from* L. *They line up, as usual.*]

CHILDREN. I'm first! Move over! What is it, Dad? Is it more
tests?

DAD [*addressing them*]. I wish to make an announcement about
your older sister.

ANNE. Dad! She hasn't even finished marking it yet.

DAD. So far as we know, your oldest sister has just completed a
perfect examination.

MISS BRILL. But, Mr. Gilbreth——

DAD [*amending his statement*]. So far as we know—yet.

CHILDREN. Hey, that's great! Wonderful! I knew it!

DAD. And it looks very much to me as though she'll graduate at the end of this semester.

ANNE [*puzzled*]. What's this about graduating?

MISS BRILL [*standing up*]. Mr. Gilbreth! You were instructed not to mention that!

DAD. You've already got her examination.

ANNE. What is this?

MISS BRILL [*her patience bursting*]. But she hasn't had the word-association test!

DAD [*imitating her*]. Well, give it to her.

MISS BRILL. Here? Now?

DAD [*seating himself comfortably in chair right of table* L C, *prepared for a treat*]. Yes, here and now. [MOTHER *stands by* DAD'S *chair.*]

MISS BRILL [*with venomous glance*]. All right. But this is very irregular.

DAD [*to* ANNE]. Are you ready now?

MARTHA. Oh, yes, she's ready!

ANNE [*very ill at ease, gulping*]. I guess so.

MISS BRILL [*taking out her pad, crossing to* ANNE *in line*]. You know how it's done. Try to answer with the word you associate. The first word. [ANNE *nods numbly as* MISS BRILL *snaps it out.*] Knife.

ANNE [*without taking a breath, words flowing together, speaking automatically*]. Stab—wound—bleed—slit—throat—murder—disembowel—scream—shriek. [MISS BRILL *stares in open-mouthed amazement. The other* CHILDREN *gulp and stare at* ANNE, *except the grinning* ERNESTINE *and* MARTHA. ANNE *stands there, expressionless.*]

MISS BRILL [*staring at* ANNE *dumbly*]. Good heavens! You must have an I.Q. higher than Nicholas Murray Butler.

ANNE [*agitatedly*]. I read a lot.

MISS BRILL [*shaking her head in wonder, taking a breath*]. Next —black.

ANNE [*as before*]. Velvet—night—pitch—tar—ebony.

MISS BRILL [*excitedly*]. Good heavens! Next—foot.

ANNE [*as before*]. Kick—shoe—walk—run—stocking—**dance.**

MISS BRILL [*quickly*]. Next—hair.

ANNE. Ribbon—hat—pigtail—shampoo—louse.

MISS BRILL [*eagerly*]. Next——

ANNE [*quickly*]. Egg—song—nest—fly—worm—perch. [*Draws in a breath and covers her mouth with her hand.*]

MISS BRILL [*startled*]. But I didn't say the word—I just said, "next."

DAD. That's true.

MISS BRILL. Let me see. [*Looks at her pad.*] The next word is "bird." You said egg—song—nest——[*With growing realization.*] So that's it! You *knew* the next word was bird.

MOTHER. How could she know?

MISS BRILL [*to* ANNE]. You did know, didn't you? [ANNE *nods slowly, miserably.*] And you knew the I.Q. exam too—[*Demanding.*]—didn't you?

ANNE. No—it was just those words. It was just a joke—— [*Swallows.*]—sort of.

MOTHER. Oh, Anne!

DAD [*deeply chagrined*]. How could you?

MISS BRILL. I see through the whole thing. [*To* CHILDREN.] You're all nasty little cheats.

DAD [*rising*]. Miss Brill!

MARTHA. I told her the words.

ERNESTINE. And me.

MISS BRILL. Yes—you all cheated.

ANNE. No—I'm the only one.

MISS BRILL. You're the only one that got caught. I see now the way you all get ahead so fast in school. I'll certainly report the whole thing to the superintendent.

ANNE. But I didn't know the test meant anything.

MISS BRILL. This ends that graduation talk. And I'll recommend that some of this grade-skipping you've done be thoroughly reviewed.

ANNE [*horrified*]. Just mine—no one else's!

MISS BRILL. The lot of you. [*Stalks out* L. *There is a long pause.*]

ANNE [*unhappily*]. Gosh, Dad—I couldn't help it.

DAD [*crossing toward her*]. What do you mean, you couldn't help it?

ANNE [*in misery*]. How could everything go so wrong? I had such a wonderful afternoon at the movie with Larry. Golly, he even asked me to a dance—and then this had to happen.

DAD. This sort of thing didn't happen till you got boys on your mind.

MOTHER [*to* DAD]. She's growing up. Other things are important, too.

DAD. Wasting time, missing dinner, perfume, painting, and now cheating on the examination. [*Absolutely determined.*] I can't have the whole program ruined by some boy-friend. This is the end of that nonsense.

ANNE. You don't realize, Dad. When you're the youngest in the class, and you feel you have to stay right up in the top bracket, sometimes you lose out on other things—like, well—leadership and sociability—going to a dance with a boy you like. [*There is a sharp knock on the door* L. ERNESTINE *crosses and opens it.*]

[LARRY, *his clothes changed, stands uncertainly in the doorway* L.]

LARRY. Hi, Ern. Is Anne ready? [ANNE *looks at* DAD. *He makes no move.*]

ANNE. Hello, Larry. [*Quietly.*] I guess I can't make it.

LARRY [*his smile fading*]. Oh . . . [*Disappointed.*] The other date came through?

ANNE. No!

LARRY [*trying to cover his disappointment*]. It's perfectly okay. After all—it's up to you. Well . . . [*Gives a somewhat half-hearted general wave, and then goes out* L.]

ANNE [*to* DAD]. I don't understand why there's only time for studies and systems and organizing things and getting more efficient.

DAD. And I don't understand——[*Shakes head.*] Never mind.

ANNE. I guess we just don't understand each other. [*Looks at* DAD *unhappily for a moment, then swallows.*] I'll give a hand in the kitchen. [*Goes out* R *quickly, in tears.*]

MOTHER. Anne . . . [*Hurries out* R.]

DAD [*regarding rest of* CHILDREN, *with a slight touch of self-justification*]. It was the only thing to do—really.

FRED. Sure.

FRANK. You're right, Dad. [*To* FRED.] We might as well finish with the dishes. [FRANK, BILL, *and* FRED *go out* R.]

MARTHA [*to* ERNESTINE]. Let's get back to the babies. [*She and* ERNESTINE *start up the stairs.*]

ERNESTINE [*as they go*]. Dad—she'll be all right. [*Goes upstairs and out with* MARTHA.]

LILLIAN. I was painting the fence. It's still not too dark.

JACKIE. I'll stir the paint. [*He and* LILLIAN *go out* L.]

DAD [*partly to self*]. I couldn't let her just run off to a dance. It's a question of the whole program. That's much more important. And time is precious.

DAN. Of course it is, Dad. [*Shrugs.*] I'd better locate that dumb dog. [*Goes out* L. DAD *is left alone on the stage.*]

DAD [*to himself*]. That's the whole thing—the time is so precious. [*Looks from side to side at empty stage.*]

[MOTHER *comes in* R.]

MOTHER [*crossing to* DAD]. Well—they're all gone. [DAD *nods. The curtain starts falling slowly.* MOTHER *smiles.*] With them all out of the living-room, it's so quiet and peaceful.

DAD. It certainly is. [*Looks about for an instant, unhappily.*] I hate it! [MOTHER *takes his arm gently.*]

CURTAIN

ACT THREE

[*The houselights fade out. Music is heard playing softly. It is "Love's Old Sweet Song" again. The dim spotlight opens up at* D R *stage, revealing* FRANK *and* ERNESTINE *standing in front of the curtain in the same position. As before, they speak in a reminiscing tone.*]

ERNESTINE [*listening*]. Is that song just in my mind, or do you hear it, too?

FRANK [*quietly*]. I hear it, too.

ERNESTINE. I don't know why—it makes me think of the afternoon Dad left for Europe.

FRANK [*remembering*]. The last time we were all together. Remember what Mother said? She was right.

ERNESTINE [*as though repeating Mother*]. "When you're all together, it's the happiest time in the world."

FRANK. She said it like she meant us to remember.

ERNESTINE. It never occurred to us Dad had any intention of dying till he was good and ready.

FRANK. I think it occurred to Anne. I think something happened that afternoon—something that made her suspect.

ERNESTINE. The way I remember, Anne spent the afternoon taking a review exam for the school board. Then she was so late coming home. Dad worried he might not even get to see her.

FRANK. She was late because of waiting for the examiner to grade her paper. She wanted something to tell Dad before he left.

ERNESTINE. The misunderstanding with Dad—Anne really took it to heart. She felt so awful.

FRANK. I think Dad felt even worse.

ERNESTINE [*agreeing*]. You could tell. When we put on the

show for him that afternoon—to give him a big send-off—he laughed and acted as though he thought it was wonderful, but —you could tell.

FRANK. He kept watching for Anne.

ERNESTINE. It was his favorite show, too—our imitation of him and Mother.

FRANK [*smiling*]. I still know it by heart.

ERNESTINE. You always took the role of Dad. I was Mother.

FRANK. Remember? [*Takes step forward.*] Ladies and gentlemen, our first guest this afternoon is Doctor Lillian Moller Gilbreth. [ERNESTINE *takes out a large, floppy hat she has been holding behind her, and puts it on.*]

ERNESTINE [*in an exaggerated imitation of Mother on a lecture platform, with exaggerated smile, waving to imaginary people in audience*]. Hello, Charlotte. So glad you could be here. Grace, I like your new hat. Why, Jennie, you've bobbed your hair. [*Then imitates lecture voice.*] I'm not going to make a speech, but I'll be glad to answer any questions.

FRANK [*as though from audience*]. Tell us, Mrs. Gilbreth, did you really want such a large family, and if so, why?

ERNESTINE. Any other questions?

FRANK. Who really wears the pants in your household?

ERNESTINE. Any other questions?

FRANK [*enthusiastically*]. Thank you, Mrs. Gilbreth, for your enlightening answers.

ERNESTINE. Our next speaker is Frank Bunker Gilbreth. [*Makes calming gesture.*] Don't be frightened now. Please keep your seats. He promised to limit himself to two hours and not to mention the "One Best Way to Do Work" more than twice in the same sentence.

FRANK [*stepping forward, pompously*]. For the purpose of convenience, I've divided my talk into thirty main headings and one hundred and seventeen sub-headings. [*Reaches into his coat, bringing forth an extremely thick manuscript.*] I commence with the first main heading——

ERNESTINE [*interrupting*]. Mr. Gilbreth—the superintendent at the factory here needs your advice at once.

FRANK. We'll all be right over.

[FRANK *imitates Dad's whistle, glancing at an imaginary stop-watch. The* CHILDREN, *all but* ANNE *and* DAN, *line up at* D R *stage. The curtain starts rising.*]

FRANK. Dear me. [*Shakes his head.*] Three seconds. [*Glares at them.*] Are you all reasonably sanitary? Is everybody dry? [CHILDREN *nod.*] All right, then, follow me.

[*The curtain is up,* DAD *and* MOTHER *are seated at the table* L C, DAD *at the right, watching the show. The* CHILDREN *get behind* FRANK *and* ERNESTINE *and lockstep into the room after them.* DAN *is waiting for them with folded arms at* C *stage. He is wearing a workman's cap. The* CHILDREN *line up in front of the sofa.*]

DAN. Mr. Gilbreth. I'm the superintendent of this factory.

FRANK. You call this a factory?

DAN [*noticing others*]. Christmas! Look what followed you in! Are those your children, or is it a picnic!

ERNESTINE [*indignantly*]. They're my children. And it's no picnic!

FRANK [*indicating* JACKIE]. How do you like my little Bolivian? Bolivians come cheaper by the dozen. Do you think I should keep them all?

DAN. I think you should keep them all home.

FRANK [*to* JACKIE, *who is sucking on his fingers*]. Jackie-boy—take the fingers out of your mouth and explain to the superintendent what's inefficient about this drill press.

JACKIE [*with exaggerated lisp*]. That thing a drill preth? Haw!

FRANK. Precisely. Lillian, explain in simple language.

LILLIAN [*taking a large lollipop out of her mouth*]. The position of the hand lever is such that there is waste motion both after transport loaded—[*Licks her lollipop.*]—and transport empty. [*Licks lollipop again.*] And the work plane of the operator is at a fatiguing level. [DAD *and* MOTHER *are enjoying this, though* DAD *pauses occasionally to look toward door* L.]

DAN. Heavens, Mr. Gilbreth! Tell your children to stop climbing over my machinery.

FRANK. They won't get hurt. They're all trained engineers. I trained them myself.

DAN [*pointing off* R]. Ohh! Look at that little Bolivian squatting over my buzz-saw! [*Covers his eyes.*] I can't watch him! Don't let him squat any lower!

FRANK [*smiling*]. The little rascal thinks it's a bicycle. Leave him alone. Children have to learn by doing. [BILL *has ducked out* R, *and there is a dying scream from him, offstage* R.]

ERNESTINE [*clucking her tongue*]. I lose more children in factories. Now, the rest of you keep away from that buzz-saw, you hear me?

FRANK. Someone make a note of that, so we'll know how many places to set for supper. [*Waves to* DAN.] Good-bye, sir . . . [CHILDREN *turn and lockstep quickly out* R. MOTHER *and* DAD *laugh and applaud.*]

[CHILDREN, *including* BILL, *re-enter* R. JACKIE *and* LILLIAN *cross to* DAD.]

JACKIE [*to* DAD]. It's your turn now!

LILLIAN. Do your one-man minstrel show!

DAD [*with glance at door* L]. No—let's wait till Anne gets home.

DAN. What if she doesn't get home in time?

MOTHER [*rising*]. She will.

MARTHA. Maybe she's having trouble with the exam.

ERNESTINE. Miss Brill probably saw to that.

DAD. Nonsense! [*Defends her.*] And if Anne does have trouble, it's just because they don't know how to put together a proper test. Some teachers just don't know their business. [*Glances at his watch.*]

JACKIE. Aren't you going to do *any* minstrel show for us?

MOTHER [*crossing toward door* R]. Your father has all sorts of last-minute things to tend to.

LILLIAN [*as they all surround* DAD]. Please—just do a little, Daddy.

DAD. Too much on my mind—really.

DAN. But we won't be seeing you for a long time.

BILL. You always do that part in the show.

DAD [*worried about Anne*]. I—I just don't much feel like——

[DAD *is cut off by the entrance of* ANNE. *She enters* L *and pauses just inside the door.*]

DAD [*greatly relieved*]. Anne! [*Rises.*]

ANNE [*subdued*]. Hello, Dad. [*Generally.*] I didn't mean to be late.

MARTHA. How'd you do?

ERNESTINE. Did you show that Miss Brill and her scl ool board?

ANNE [*coming to left of table* L C]. They haven't finished marking my paper. I tried to explain I was in a hurry. [MOTHER *comes behind sofa.*]

DAD [*determined*]. I know you did fine. [*Concerned.*] But you took so long—I was beginning to worry.

ANNE [*upset*]. Dad—it was a hard exam. I don't know *how* I did. [*Anxiously.*] I tried my best, though—my really best.

DAD [*shaking off any concern*]. 'Course you did. [*Wanting her to understand.*] I was just afraid you wouldn't get back in time. [*Looks at her a moment, then takes* C *stage, in minstrel manner.*] Mistah Bones—I say, Mistah Bones——

JACKIE [*delightedly*]. Yea, Dad!

DAD [*continuing with exaggerated minstrel manner*]. Does you know how you gets de water in de watermelon? [*Reverses position and changes tone to answer.*] No—how does you get de water in de watermelon? [*Back to original pose.*] Why, you plants dem in de spring! [*Slaps his knee.*] Yak! Yak!

DAN. More, Dad!

MOTHER. Now, that's enough.

DAD [*as before*]. Does you know Isabelle? [*Reverses position.*] Isabelle? [*Back to first position.*] Why, sho! Is-a-belle necessary on a bicycle? [*Slaps his knee.*] Yak! Yak!

[MRS. FITZGERALD *enters* R.]

MRS. FITZGERALD [*to* DAD, *coming* D R C]. I set out a snack for you. [*Sternly.*] No decent food on trains. [*Then, to* CHILDREN.] There's ice cream and cookies for the rest of you. [*Goes out* R.]

CHILDREN [*the younger ones*]. Hooray, ice cream! Cookies! I'm starved! Me, too!

DAD [*with mock severity*]. I don't know about this. When it comes to ice cream, you're right on the job, but when it comes to a project, you're slow as molasses.

JACKIE. Hey, Dad!

LILLIAN. Please!

DAD [*with wink at* MOTHER]. What do you say, Boss?

MOTHER [*imitating* DAD'S *minstrel man*]. Did you say mo-lasses, Mistah Bones? Why, I ain't had no-lasses—come long, chillen. [MOTHER, LILLIAN, BILL, JACKIE, FRANK, DAN, *and* FRED *troop out* R, *leaving* DAD, ANNE, MARTHA, *and* ERNESTINE *on the stage.*]

DAD [*to* ANNE, *not wanting to reveal quite how much it matters, but feeling he should say something*]. I'm glad you finished up and got home. [MARTHA *and* ERNESTINE *sit on sofa.*]

ANNE. Oh, I'd have been home in time, anyway—I mean, I wouldn't let anything——

DAD. I'll bet you made them feel foolish for insisting on a review examination.

ANNE [*worried*]. I don't know. [*Sits left of table* L C.]

DAD [*decisively, standing above table* L C]. Of course you did. All you had to do was get the foolishnes out of your mind so you could do your best.

ANNE. Dad, I did my best, but—[*Swallows.*]—I haven't got the foolishness out of my mind.

DAD [*in sharper tone*]. Anne——

ERNESTINE. Aw, Dad.

MARTHA. She's been studying herself sick.

ANNE. I can't help it.

DAD [*disappointed, crossing* R]. I can't understand why you haven't more sense. [*Goes out* R.]

ANNE [*crossing after him*]. Dad . . .

MARTHA. I'm glad I'm not the oldest. By the time he gets to us, things will be taken for granted.

ANNE [*bothered, puzzled, coming back to* C *stage*]. I don't see why Dad cares so much.

ERNESTINE. Sometimes it seems like he's the strictest father in town.

ANNE [*hesitantly*]. Were there any calls for me—or anything?

MARTHA [*nodding*]. Larry.

ANNE [*eagerly*]. Did he say anything? [MARTHA *shakes her head*. ANNE *continues suspiciously*.] Did *you* say anything?

MARTHA. A little. [*Shrugs*.] I helped your cause.

ANNE [*worried*]. How?

MARTHA [*rising, moving toward her*]. I didn't let him think you'd just been studying all the time for an exam—that's so drab. [*Wisely*.] I gave him something colorful to think about.

ANNE [*holding herself back, urgently*]. What?

MARTHA [*what else*]. About all your other dates.

ANNE. No!

MARTHA [*nodding eagerly*]. I'm not so dumb.

ERNESTINE [*to* MARTHA]. Any time "Motorcycle Mac" calls, just keep your brilliance to yourself!

MARTHA. What's the matter?

ANNE. Now he'll think——Gosh, Mart!

MARTHA [*with hopeless shrug*]. I can't help it if neither of you understand men. [*Sound of motorcycle begins fading in*.]

ERNESTINE [*hearing sound*]. Don't understand men—watch how I handle Mac. [*Rises, and they face door* L.]

MARTHA. He won't even slow down.

ERNESTINE [*knowingly*]. He'd better.

ANNE. What do you mean?

ERNESTINE. You know where he swings in with the motorcycle? [*They nod*.] This is the last time he swings. [*To* ANNE.] You gave me the idea.

ANNE. What idea?

ERNESTINE. Nails and broken glass!

ANNE [*horrified*]. I was joking!

MARTHA. We'd better warn him! [*Sound of motorcycle is right outside door L.*]

ANNE [*hopefully*]. I think he missed! [*Sound reaches its peak. There is an explosion, a sound of brakes, skidding, and then a crash.*]

ERNESTINE. Got him! [*They rush to door L.*]

MARTHA [*as they look out*]. My gosh.

ANNE. It's—it's *Larry!*

ERNESTINE. What's Larry doing on Mac's motorcycle?

ANNE [*as she looks at him*]. Oh, no!

MARTHA. The poor guy!

[*LARRY enters L. He has obviously been in a smash-up. He carries a nail-studded piece of board in his hand.*]

ANNE. Larry——

LARRY [*indignantly, holding up board*]. Whose idea was this? [*Looks from one to the other.*]

ERNESTINE [*technically accurate*]. The idea was Anne's.

LARRY. Not enough to give me the run-around! Now you're trying to kill me!

ANNE. Kill *you!*

ERNESTINE. You've got it all wrong.

MARTHA. Really!

LARRY [*waving board at ANNE, as he backs her to C stage*]. People get put in jail for things like this.

ANNE. You're not going to get me put in jail?

LARRY [*indignantly*]. Well . . . [*Softening.*] No.

ANNE [*miserably*]. You can if you want to.

LARRY [*shocked at thought*]. Why would I want you in jail? Even if you are running around with college boys while I thought you were studying. [*ANNE turns towards MARTHA, accusingly.*] Even if you have accepted three fraternity pins at the same time.

MARTHA [*hurrying to door* R]. My ice cream is probably melting
—if you'll excuse me. [*Eases out* R.]

LARRY [*bewildered*]. I still don't see why you put nails in the
drive!

ANNE. I didn't. I might have suggested the idea once—as a joke,
but——

ERNESTINE [*quickly, moving* R]. My ice cream—it's probably
melting, too. [*Hurries out* R.]

LARRY [*reproachfully*]. I thought you were so different.

ANNE. I *am* different—I guess.

LARRY. I used to think so—I used to think you were sincere, and
knew about lots of things. [*Worried.*] I borrowed that motorcycle. [*Crosses* L.] I'd better see how much damage was done.

ANNE [*hopefully, moving toward him*]. Can I help?

LARRY. You've done enough. [*Goes out* L. ANNE *looks after him
unhappily.*]

[MOTHER *enters* R.]

MOTHER [*coming to right end of sofa*]. Aren't you going to eat
any ice cream, dear?

ANNE [*shaking her head, choked*]. I don't have much appetite.

MOTHER. Are you worried about the test?

ANNE [*crossing toward sofa*]. The test and—everything.

MOTHER [*smiling*]. That boy? [ANNE *nods.*] Anything else?

ANNE. Dad. [*Sits on sofa.*]

MOTHER. You're worried about Dad? [*Sits beside her.*]

ANNE [*seriously concerned*]. We used to understand each other
so well. Now it seems like we don't understand each other at
all.

MOTHER. Your father tries to do so much. Sometimes he gets
impatient.

ANNE [*puzzled*]. Why's he in such a hurry for us? Why doesn't
he want us spending time with boys—or anything like that?
It seems like we have to make every minute count.

MOTHER [*pausing, then speaking, troubled*]. He might have a
reason.

ANNE. What, Mother?

MOTHER [*smiling*]. He might want to get as many of his dozen as possible through school. You especially. You're the oldest.

ANNE. But we'll all get through school. Why the hurry?

MOTHER. After all, Dad's along in his fifties.

ANNE [*laughing*]. Dad's young!

MOTHER [*distrubed, rising, moving toward table* L C]. People get things wrong with them—things like—heart trouble.

ANNE [*after a pause, speaking quietly*]. Is that why Doctor Burton's always coming over?

MOTHER. It's nothing for you to get excited about.

ANNE [*rising, crossing to her*]. Mother, does Dad have heart trouble?

MOTHER [*unsure of herself*]. You see . . .

ANNE [*urgently*]. Does he?

MOTHER [*looking at* ANNE *for a moment*]. You're so eager to grow up.

ANNE [*realizing*]. Mother! . . .

MOTHER [*her arms around* ANNE]. Of course he wants you all getting ahead as fast as possible. Of course he wants everything efficient and organized.

ANNE [*in tears*]. Oh, Mother!

MOTHER. Shh. Now you're thinking it's much worse than it is.

ANNE. If I'd known . . .

MOTHER. There, darling. It isn't that bad.

[DAD *enters* R. *He has a large piece of paper in his hands.* JACKIE *follows him in.* ANNE *gets control of herself.*]

DAD [*coming to* C *with* JACKIE]. Boss—I forgot to put up the cross-section graph.

MOTHER. I can show them all later.

ANNE. What is it, Dad?

DAD. A thousand lines long and a thousand lines wide. That makes exactly a million little squares.

JACKIE. A million!

DAD. You hear people talk a lot about big numbers these days, but not many people know what an awful lot a million is. [*Indicates chart.*] You're going to see it every day.

JACKIE. Do you have a million dollars, Daddy?

DAD [*shaking his head*]. No—I have a million children instead. Somewhere along the line, a man has to choose between the two.

ANNE [*taking graph*]. I'll put it up later, Dad. I could explain what it means. [*Places paper on table* L C.]

DAD [*pleased*]. Later this afternoon. [*To* JACKIE.] Don't you like ice cream any more?

JACKIE. Me! [*Zips back out* R. DAD *smiles, then glances at his watch again.*]

DAD. Mrs. Piper—come up with me while I say good-bye to the babies.

MOTHER [*going upstairs with him*]. What toys are you going to bring back for them, Mr. Piper—slide rules?

DAD [*smiling*]. Why, Mrs. Piper, what a good suggestion! [ANNE *looks after them as* DAD *and* MOTHER *go out.*]

[*The door* L *opens and* LARRY *enters.*]

LARRY [*to* ANNE]. Just the tire and a bent mud-guard. [ANNE *is still looking after* DAD.] It could be much worse. [*Pauses at door* L.]

ANNE [*focusing on him*]. What?

LARRY [*slightly irritated*]. The motorcycle.

ANNE. Oh.

LARRY. They cost money, you know.

ANNE [*subdued and preoccupied, moving toward sofa*]. Maybe Ern and I could pay for the damage—gradually.

LARRY [*regarding her for a moment*]. It was pretty old and beat up, anyway.

ANNE [*her mind still on Dad*]. But whatever it costs——

LARRY. Anne! . . . [*Crosses toward her.*]

ANNE. Yes?

LARRY [*indignantly*]. How come you spend all your time with college boys when you're supposed to be studying? I didn't think you were that kind of girl.

ANNE [*more definitely aware of him now*]. I'm not.

LARRY. You don't have to pretend with me.

[BILL *enters* R.]

ANNE. I'm not pretending. [*Impulsively takes his hands.*] I wouldn't pretend with you. [*Worried about Dad.*] I don't think people should pretend with people.

LARRY [*sincerely*]. I don't either. [BILL *has been shaking his head at their hand-holding.*]

BILL. So you're at it again! [*They jerk their hands apart.* BILL *goes on up the stairs and out.*] Shocking!

LARRY [*looking after* BILL]. He certainly has a wonderful sense of timing.

ANNE [*concerned*]. I hope he doesn't upset Dad. Larry—Dad's leaving—and all—I'd better see if I can help with things.

LARRY. Sure. I'll get along. [*Hesitates.*] You don't really have three fraternity pins? I mean, I wouldn't think your dad——

ANNE. Of course not. [*With glance at stairs.*] I won't have time for any nonsense like that.

LARRY. What do you mean?

ANNE [*moving to* D R C]. Sometimes a person has to push ahead with important things—sometimes there're reasons.

LARRY [*hurt, crossing toward her*]. Going to a dance with me—that wouldn't be important?

ANNE [*unhappily*]. You don't understand—I didn't understand, myself. [*Doorbell rings lightly. They are not aware of it.*]

LARRY [*puzzled*]. What?

ANNE. Reasons. I can't explain. There's so much I'll have to do. I won't have much time.

[DAD *enters on the stairs and starts down slowly.* LARRY *and* ANNE *are not aware of him.*]

LARRY. Not even for the Senior Prom?

ANNE. You mean—you're asking? [LARRY *nods.*] Gosh, Larry, I——[*Shakes her head.*] But it wouldn't be right. I mean, with Dad away—things have to be pushed along.

LARRY. You won't go?

ANNE [*swallowing*]. I can't.

DAD [*coming down*]. Don't you answer the doorbell, any more?

ANNE [*starting*]. Dad! I didn't hear it.

DAD. You weren't listening.

LARRY. Hello, Mr. Gilbreth.

DAD [*nodding to him, then to* ANNE]. I thought you *wanted* to go to a dance?

ANNE. I do, but——

DAD [*deeply pleased with her, but holding it down*]. Sounds like I have an eldest daughter—just about grown up. [*Doorbell rings again. This time it is clearly audible. Crosses to door* L.] I wonder . . . [*He is startled as he opens door.*] Good heavens!

[MISS BRILL *comes in* L.]

DAD. Good afternoon. [MISS BRILL *nods shortly.*]

[MOTHER *enters on stairs.*]

MOTHER. Who is it? [*Sees* MISS BRILL.] Oh. [*Starts down stairs and comes to right of table* L C.]

DAD [*to* MISS BRILL]. Won't you sit down?

MISS BRILL [*standing*]. I understand you're leaving, so I'll be brief.

ANNE [*moving in front of sofa*]. Did you mark my paper?

MISS BRILL. The superintendent marked it himself.

[FRED *and* JACKIE *enter* R *and move* D R.]

ANNE [*anxiously*]. Yes?

MISS BRILL. It wasn't my idea to come here.

MOTHER. About what?

MISS BRILL. The examination.

ANNE. Please—did I pass?

DAD. Let's have it. [*Irritated.*] I catch a train in a few minutes.

MISS BRILL. It's obvious to me she cheated again.

DAD [*sharply*]. *Miss Brill!*

ANNE. You know I didn't. You watched me every minute.

MISS BRILL. I don't claim to know *how*.

DAD. Get to the point. I'm in a hurry.

MISS BRILL. That's why I was sent right over.

MOTHER. So——

MISS BRILL. She may fool other people, but she doesn't fool me.

ANNE [*demanding*]. What was my mark?

MISS BRILL. I'm getting to it.

DAD. Did she pass?

MISS BRILL. Yes.

DAD. Was it a good paper?

MISS BRILL. Yes.

DAD. Was anything *wrong* with her paper?

MISS BRILL. No.

FRED. Yea, Anne!

MOTHER [*delightedly, hugging* ANNE]. Darling!

DAD. There's no more question about when she graduates?

MISS BRILL. That's what I was told to tell you. I was told to say she's to graduate the end of this semester.

DAD [*slapping knee*]. By jingo, I knew it!

LARRY [*to* ANNE]. Hey, that's swell!

MISS BRILL. Now, if you'll excuse me——

DAD. Thank you, Miss Brill.

FRED [*unable to repress himself, to* MISS BRILL]. How much is nineteen times thirty-six?

MISS BRILL [*backing away*]. Really . . .

FRED [*as she retreats toward door*]. Nineteen times thirty-six?

MISS BRILL. *I'm* not taking a test. Good day! [*Hurries out* L. JACKIE *rushes to door* L.]

JACKIE [*shouting after her*]. It's six hundred eighty-four! [ALL *laugh.*]

[MARTHA *and* ERNESTINE *enter* R *and join* FRED D R.]

MOTHER [*to* ANNE]. I'm so glad!

ANNE. I was worried.

DAD. Nonsense! [*To* MARTHA *and* ERNESTINE, *moving to* C.] Your sister did wonderfully!

ERNESTINE [*overjoyed*]. Snake hips!

MARTHA [*shrugging*]. Knew she would.

DAD [*chortling*]. Insisted she take the exam—forced it on her.

ANNE. I didn't really cheat that first time, Dad.

DAD. I know. Mart and Ernestine already explained. [*Laughs.*] I haven't felt so good in years.

LARRY. Anne, I have to get on home.

ANNE. I'm glad you came over.

LARRY. About the prom?

DAD. What I started to say before I was interrupted by Miss Brill —[*To* ANNE.]—it seems to me you're beginning to grow up.

MOTHER [*to* DAD]. She is. More than you think.

DAD. And when a girl begins to grow up, it doesn't hurt if she goes to a few dances.

ANNE [*unbelievingly*]. It's all right? [DAD *nods. She is overjoyed.*] I won't let it ever interfere with my studies or anything, Dad—honestly!

DAD [*smiling*]. Easy, now—I believe you.

LARRY [*to* DAD]. I hope you have a nice trip—and don't worry about Anne going to the prom, or anything.

DAD. You bet I won't. I'm sending Bill right along with you.

LARRY [*laughing*]. Sure thing. [*Pauses, impressed.*] It's really something the way you've taught them.

JACKIE [*helpfully*]. Would you like to learn how to multiply two-digit numbers in your head?

MOTHER. Never mind, Jackie.

LARRY [*with general wave of hand*]. Good-bye. [*To* ANNE.] Be seeing you. [*Moves to door* L.]

ANNE [*repeating words with her lips, but without making a sound*]. Be seeing you. [LARRY *goes out* L. DAD *looks at his watch again.*]

MOTHER. It's late. [DAD *nods.*] I've had Frank put your bags in the car already.

DAD. Good. [*Looks at them all.*] By jingo!

[DAD *fumbles with his stop-watch, takes it out, and then whistles assembly.* LILLIAN, DAN, *and* FRANK *rush in* R. BILL *comes down the stairs. The* CHILDREN *form their line.* DAD *clicks watch.*]

DAD. Nine seconds. [*Looks them over.*] That's very good. I—I have to hurry.

JACKIE [*almost in tears*]. Daddy!

MOTHER. Hush.

DAD. No need for any last-minute nonsense now. You know your jobs and responsibilities. My last official act before leaving is to nominate your mother for chairman of the family council. All those in favor? [*There is a chorus of "Ayes."*] She is now your new chairman. [*Puts his arm about* MOTHER.]

CHILDREN [*anxiously*]. Do you have to go now? Wait till to-morrow. Could I go with you? Write us often. Send post cards. We'll write, too—every day! Every day!

DAD [*glancing at watch*]. Here now . . .

MOTHER. Your father has to hurry.

ANNE [*stepping from line*]. Dad—before you go—there is just one thing I don't understand.

DAD [*fondly*]. Just one?

ANNE [*nodding*]. I think maybe I know why you want us to get ahead—but everything you do—all your work to save time for everybody—the thing I don't understand is—what do you want to save time for?

DAD [*after slight pause*]. For work, if you love that best. For ed-ucation, for beauty, or art. [*Smiles.*] For mumblety-peg, if that's where your heart lies. [*Looks from face to face of* CHIL-DREN.] It's for where your heart lies—that's what you save time for. [*He has his arms around several of the* CHILDREN.]

MOTHER [*smiling at* DAD]. Right now is the happiest time in the world. [*There is a pause.*]

DAD [*breaking pause, energetically*]. No waving good-bye non-sense. Get along with things. [*Kisses* MOTHER. *Then to* CHIL-DREN.] And, by jingo, behave yourselves! [*Turns and goes out* L. ANNE *has her arm around* MOTHER. *The sound of "Love's Old Sweet Song," playing softly, fades in.* MOTHER *and* ANNE *are looking off after* DAD.]

FRANK. Fred—get your mother a chair. All of you—arrange yourselves for a meeting. [FRED *brings chair* D L *to* C. *Then they take their regular positions, except* ANNE, *who still stands with her arm about* MOTHER.] Mother—Mr. Chairman—Mr. Chairman——

ANNE [*gently tugging at her*]. Mother . . . [MOTHER *looks around. They are waiting for her. She stands by chair.* ANNE *takes her place by desk* D R. *Curtain starts falling slowly.*]

MOTHER. Like all families, we have to get on with the business before us. [*Raps on chair.*] I now call this family council to order. [*The curtain is down.*]

CURTAIN

WHAT PEOPLE ARE SAYING about *Cheaper by the Dozen*.

"We did this play seven years ago and still love it! It's a real audience pleaser and a great adaptation of the book. Love having a single set."   *Ana Clark, Quo Vadis Players, Garland, Texas*

"What a wonderful play! It's so nice to find a play with several characters and they all have fun moments on stage. I always have to do large-cast plays and all my kids want to be in the play. This play fits the bill."
        Charla Little, Red Oak High School, Red Oak, Texas

"Everyone associated with our production loved working on this play. The show offers just the right blend of comedy and melancholy. The whole cast and crew began to feel and behave like one big extension of the Gilbreth family."   *Alan J. Davino,*
        Catskill Theatre Works, Inc., Delhi, N.Y.

"*Cheaper by the Dozen* is definitely one of the most exciting and delightful plays I've ever directed. It was well received by the cast and audience. I'm looking forward to someday directing its sequel, *Belles on Their Toes*."   *Kim Dreschler,*
        H.O.M.E. School, Lake Balboa, Calif.

"This is an easy show to cast and block. The stage directions are marvelous and the sound effects tape was especially helpful."
        [Mr. or Ms.] Lair, New London Community School,
        New London, Iowa

(continued on following page)

"*Cheaper by the Dozen* was a great show—lots of fun to produce. It is the perfect mix of simple sets, funny lines, and yet, deep meaning."   *Joyanne Krause,*
                    Trinity International University, Deerfield, Ill.

"*Cheaper by the Dozen* was a charming, hilarious comedy with some poignant moments we could all relate to, even in this modern age. It was well received by audience and cast alike and is our favorite production to date. Everyone loved the period costumes and sayings of the day."   *Jane Savage,*
                    Santa Rosa Christian School, Santa Rosa, Calif.

"Wonderfully fun to produce. *Cheaper* gave our younger actors the opportunity to play characters that were not 'animals.' So good we intend to do [the sequel] *Belles on Their Toes* next year."   *Jonathan Fly, HCT Productions, Hutchinson, Kan.*